CASE STUDIES IN
CULTURAL ANTHROPOLOGY

GENERAL EDITORS
George and Louise Spindler
STANFORD UNIVERSITY

THE MBUTI PYGMIES

Change and Adaptation

Mbuti hunting camp

THE MBUTI PYGMIES

Change and Adaptation

By

COLIN M. TURNBULL

George Washington University

HOLT, RINEHART AND WINSTON

NEW YORK   CHICAGO   SAN FRANCISCO   PHILADELPHIA

MONTREAL   TORONTO   LONDON   SYDNEY   TOKYO

MEXICO CITY   RIO DE JANEIRO   MADRID

Library of Congress Cataloging in Publication Data

Turnbull, Colin M.
  The Mbuti pygmies.

  (Case studies in cultural anthropology)
  Bibliography: p. 159
  1. Bambute. 2. Acculturation—Zaire—Case studies.
I. Title. II. Series.
DT650.B36T88 1983   306'.09675'1   82–21332
ISBN 0-03-061537-2

CBS COLLEGE PUBLISHING
Holt, Rinehart and Winston
The Dryden Press
Saunders College Publishing

Foreword

ABOUT THE SERIES

These case studies in cultural anthropology are designed to bring to students, in beginning and intermediate courses in the social sciences, insights into the richness and complexity of human life as it is lived in different ways and in different places. They are written by men and women who have lived in the societies they write about and who are professionally trained as observers and interpreters of human behavior. The authors are also teachers, and in writing their books they have kept the students who will read them foremost in their minds. It is our belief that when an understanding of way of life very different from one's own is gained, abstractions and generalizations about social structure, cultural values, subsistence techniques, and the other universal categories of human social behavior become meaningful.

ABOUT THE AUTHOR

Colin Turnbull was born in England in 1924. He studied music and philosophy in both England and India before returning to Oxford University and turning to anthropology, which he pursued there under Professor E. E. Evans-Pritchard. Most of his field work (six major trips) has been in Africa, and his work with museums and universities has also largely been in connection with African studies. More recently, however, his concern has been with the application of his exotic studies to the better understanding of typical American social institutions such as tourism, and of issues of major social concern such as capital punishment and the related problems of stress, security, and rehabilitation in our prison system. He combines teaching at George Washington University with writing, field research, farming and, whenever possible, making music.

ABOUT THE BOOK

This case study provides a unique opportunity for readers to learn not only about a most interesting people, the Mbuti pygmies of the Ituri forest, but also about changes in a very significant part of Africa from the colonial era to the present. It is not often that a single book will cover so great a time span of such importance to the shape of the modern world. Nor is it often that we can receive the thoughtful analysis of a senior anthropologist who has done repeated field work in such an area over such a period of time in the format of a case study. Colin Turnbull is well known for his writings on the Mbuti, some of which are listed under Recommended Reading at the end of this study. He has also worked with and written about the Ik, a hunting and gathering people who, like the Mbuti, were subject to massive changes in their ecology, but who reacted quite differently.

This case study weaves a number of themes together. The major features of the Mbuti way of life and the sanctuary furnished them by the great Ituri forest, their existence under colonialism and their relations with the villagers, peoples with wholly different customs, values, and adaptations, whom the Mbuti regarded with mixed feeling, the destructive and cruel years of war, when deeper penetrations were made into the Mbuti world, and the situation now, since independence—all of this is woven together in one complex but very understandable, and at times quite moving, analysis. The past, the present, and the future flow together, much as they would, it seems, for the Mbuti.

The author can write as he has because his experience with the Mbuti, and with the villagers, is deep, prolonged, and repetitive. Returning to the scene of one's field work repeatedly, with significant intervals in between, gives one a perspective that cannot be obtained in any other way. One's initial interpretations are seen in a new light, and new interpretations, of both old and new data, begin to emerge quite naturally. This case study exhibits the benefits of this experience to good advantage.

GEORGE AND LOUISE SPINDLER
General Editors

Calistoga, California

Acknowledgements

It is conventional for anthropologists, like others, to express their gratitude and indebtedness to those who have helped them with the study they are now publishing. Since this study deals with social change and adaptation it seems appropriate to draw attention to the way in which any one author changes and adapts in his practice of acknowledgement. In successive works the same scholars may be thanked repeatedly, but whereas some anthropologists express gratitude to their parents, usually in their first publication, acknowledgement of this debt (which surely is general and enduring) is seldom repeated. Similarly with expressions of gratitude to the populations among whom we have worked. And actually, if we really wanted to be as meticulous as we pretend to be in our scholarship, should we not only publicly recognize those from whom we have learned, but also the sources of their abilities and qualities? It might be going a little far to express our gratitude to *their* mothers and fathers, but it does seem relevant that we should recognize that whatever benefit we might have drawn from Radcliffe-Brown, say, is due in part at least to the benefit and inspiration *he* drew from Heraclitus. But then Heraclitus is dead, and it seems that we feel most constrained to thank those who are still alive, and influential.

Unless acknowledgements serve the clear academic purpose of helping toward a better evaluation of the work to follow, they are better omitted. And if we were to undertake that scholarly task with any seriousness then we would have to preface each book we write with a philosophical discourse.

I myself have gone through the usual sequence, at different times thanking parents, teachers, friends, colleagues, whole populations, and selected individuals from those populations. I doubt if any of these efforts to express indebtedness succeeded, either as such or in the more serious business of placing the study in its proper academic context. And since I myself am now a good deal older than I was when I began writing, my own sensibilities have changed. Many of those who taught me the most are dead. And it is increasingly obvious to me that the influences bearing on my work and writing are so complex and in such constant flux that dealing with them responsibly would take a book in itself, and a rather dull one at that.

So I am persuaded by the spirit of change and adaptation, which to my mind is one of the most dynamic forces in our personal and social lives, to thank those who leave me behind, pushing further ahead than I could ever have done, and in directions that often I had not even considered. At this very moment, in the northeastern corner of the Ituri Forest, there is a whole team at work under the direction of Irven DeVore. So far I have learned little in general and nothing specific as to their discoveries, but whatever these discoveries are, they will be both valid and valuable, however remote or close their findings may be to my own of another

vii

time and another part of the same forest. And only a few years back, arriving just as I was leaving from my last field trip to the Ituri (1970–72), came another team, from Japan, led by Professor J. Itani, with formidable yet friendly scholars such as Tadashi Tanno, Reizo Harako, and Mitzuo Ichikawa, all of whom, jointly and severally, went far beyond anything done by any of us who had gone before. Now *there* is real cause for gratitude, and if acknowledgement is to be made, perhaps it is best made to those who will follow still further in the future, adding yet more to our knowledge and understanding: In other words, let us make an acknowledgement of our own inadequacy.

Special thanks are due to the National Science Foundation, which, under Grant #GS 36442 and through the cooperation of Hofstra University, made possible the research undertaken by Dr. Towles and myself, from 1970 to 1973, during which much of the following material was collected. Our sponsors allowed a radical change of research objectives in midstream, committing themselves to humanity as well as science.

Contents

CASE STUDIES IN

CULTURAL ANTHROPOLOGY

GENERAL EDITORS
George and Louise Spindler
STANFORD UNIVERSITY

––––––––––––

THE MBUTI PYGMIES

Change and Adaptation

Introduction

The word *pygmy* generally gives rise to so many misconceptions that I prefer to avoid it as much as possible. Yet the same word inevitably arouses curiosity, interest, even fascination—attitudes not to be lightly dismissed by any writer who wants to be read! The main reasons that I dislike the term are two: *Pygmies* refers to populations of short stature; four feet six inches or below is the generally accepted figure. Such populations are spread throughout the world, and while their historical and genetic relationship with each other is a matter of question, the cultural factors are such that each population deserves to be treated in its own right. By using the term *Mbuti* to refer to the hunters of the Ituri Forest, in Zaïre, I hope to avoid suggesting that whatever I have to say about one discrete African population, which happens to be "pygmy," has any necessary bearing on any other pygmy population, in Africa or elsewhere. For the cultural or social anthropologist to lump populations together merely because of the size of its people is plainly ludicrous. My second objection to the word is that it invites the assumption that height is a significant factor, whereas, in the Ituri, it is of remarkable insignificance to both the Mbuti and their neighbors, the taller Africans who live around them.

The already well-established terminology led me to fall into the trap early on, when I referred to the two major forest populations as "negroes" (a then acceptable physiological designation) and "pygmies," as though physiology were an important factor. However, a much more significant difference between the two neighboring populations, which we shall be discussing here, is primarily ideological and economic. The one population, the Mbuti pygmies, consider themselves as "children of the forest" (*bamiki ba'ndura*) and live in close symbiosis with the forest as nomadic hunter-gatherers, dwelling in small temporary camps, the very kinship constitution of which is constantly changing with changing location. The other population is made up of a number of different immigrant tribes who are either farmers or fishers, who live in semipermanent villages of relatively fixed patrilineal composition, and who generally view themselves as being in opposition to the forest world rather than as a part of it. The relative size of the human body is of little significance when considering these cultural and social factors.

The various pygmy populations of Africa are scattered throughout the equatorial belt, wherever the primary rain forest still exists. There are some suggestions that they might at one time have been related to the Koisan ("Bushman") populations of southern Africa, but this, like most questions of origin, is a matter of contro-

1

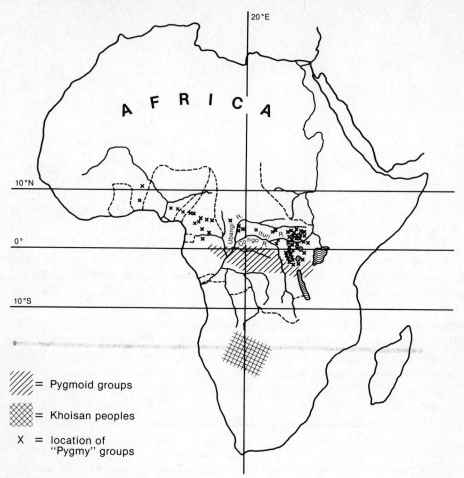

Map 1: *Extent of personal knowledge of "pygmy" groups according to accounts heard* in situ *and through personal contact made during the 1957/58 field trip. This does not include the large number of pygmoid groups known as Twa and Tswa, who live mainly outside the forest to the south and southeast, and who have little in common with the Mbuti in terms of culture.*

versy and need not concern us here. Like height, the question of "pygmy" origins is a red herring for us in our particular endeavor. What *is* significant is that both populations of the forest *believe* that the hunters, the pygmy groups, are the original inhabitants, and thus not only have certain rights, but possess certain powers that the immigrants do not have.

The Ituri Forest, in the very geographical center of Africa, may seem not only remote in distance from our own world, but remote in significance, and the lives of its still largely traditional populations may seem almost irrelevant to us. That is not so. We have much to learn from them, not the least being how two populations that are visibly distinct as well as culturally and socially opposed to each

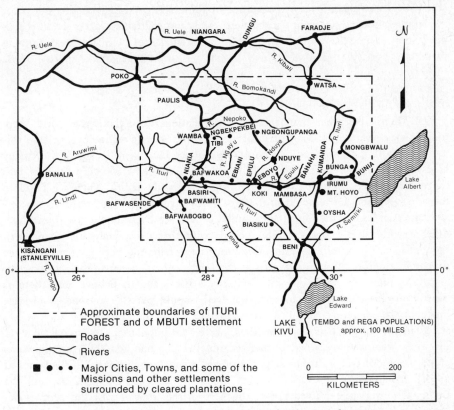

Map 2: Boundaries of Ituri Forest and Mbuti settlement.

other have managed to arrive at an effective, nonviolent, nonhostile relationship that works to the advantage of both. Other points of relevance will emerge as we go along, so while reading about "others," let us not forget that we may be learning about ourselves.

This is true even when considering the exotic environment, the rain forest, in which these peoples live. The area known best to me covers about fifty thousand square miles, lying mostly just north of the equator. Its trees soar up to well over a hundred feet in height, some approaching two hundred, and the canopy shelters most of the forest floor from any direct sunlight so that it remains cool and moist, whereas the villages where the farmers live, where the forest has been cut down, are hot, dry, and dusty much of the time. We induce changes in our own environment, consciously and otherwise, and in this way we also induce changes in lifestyle leading to differing preferences, oppositions, and even to mutual misunderstandings and hostility. So while reading about a people living in a tropical rain forest, we should keep in mind that what is significant is not the difference in the environment so much as the similarity (or difference) in the way we all relate to and adapt to our divers environments.

It is the exotic world of the "pygmy" that has fascinated people for centuries;

not just the strange (to us) appearance of these short-statured people, but more the strange, isolated, to many "forbidding" and "impenetrable" forest world that is their home. These are all understandable ethnocentricities, with no great harm in them. But underlying all this curiosity is perhaps the most significant factor of all, for our fascination is also with the fact that in this exotic, tropical rain forest a people seem to live today much as they lived thousands of years ago, with a cultural form that is essentially pre-stone age.

The Mbuti, like other hunter-gatherer populations throughout the world, seem to have mastered the knack of survival despite their archaic technology, or, and this is the nagging question, could it be *because* of it? Unwilling to admit this, many have deemed these remnant populations stagnant, though their very survival into the twentieth century is proof of enduring vigor and vitality. Then we fall into the other trap and are tempted to think of such "primitive" populations as "stable," and take peoples like the Mbuti as examples of how *we* lived thousands of years ago.

In a world that is increasingly rocked by potentially cataclysmic changes in economic, political, religious, and domestic life, where the very changes that are sought so ardently by some are seen as threats by others, we are prone to long for a mythical state of being we call "stability." We come to believe that there is actually an ideal state, which, once achieved, should persist, immune to change. Much of the glamour that until recently attached to the "primitive" way of life rested in the mistaken notion that there were vast populations, scattered all over the world, that had remained unchanged not just for hundreds but for thousands of years. Notions of a "timeless past," of an "unchanging way of life" abounded in popular accounts of exotic societies in South America, Africa, Asia, and the Pacific. The romance derived not so much from the life-styles of the peoples described as from the myth of timelessness and absence of change. It suggested, if not immortality or eternity, at least a greater degree of social longevity than seemed likely for western civilization. It linked us to a past more remote than anything we had thought possible, and when we coupled that antiquarian pride with all the pride and self-satisfaction we felt in the achievements of modern science, invoking the concept of progress, our existence suddenly assumed new and greater significance.

This was all rather unfortunate, since the sense of well-being (if not complacency) that it established was built on very shaky ground. We have since come to recognize that the very change that alarms us as it affects and often drastically modifies the patterns of our daily lives, is both natural and essential, inevitable and functional. It is nothing new in the history of this planet, let alone in the history of mankind. What *is* new and what *might* indeed be dysfunctional, if not exactly cataclysmic, is not the fact of change, but the rapidity with which it comes and goes, and the almost aggressive nature of its onslaught. What is also new is that whereas much of the change that has always characterized human society and social organization was in the past due to "natural" causes (environmental change, population growth and movement, pestilence and disease, and so forth), many, if not most of the dramatic changes that now confront us are due to conscious human intervention: technological, intellectual, social, political, and economic. Theoretically, of course, that means that the process should be reversible, and that we should equally consciously be able to slow down and redirect the course of social change.

However, even though this is well-enough known to all of us, a strange kind of conservatism makes us wish that it were not so, or at least not so *much* so. The "primitive" retains his hold on our fascination, apparently as enviable in light of our contemporary knowledge of his own involvement in an ever-changing world as he was when we thought of him as timeless and unchanging.

Of course social and cultural anthropologists do not go into the field to satisfy such yearnings for immortality; we study other societies in order to find out what we can about whatever general principles of social organization are at work in all human society. If we have our heads about us, we go into the field hoping to learn something about "them," but confidently expecting to learn a great deal more about "us." And that is how it should be. Those of us who have the privilege of returning to the field more than once have the incalculable advantage of learning by personal experience something of the process of change as it affects the small-scale societies we traditionally study.

I was first among the Mbuti pygmies of the Ituri Forest, in what was then the Belgian Congo, in 1951. I went back for something over a year in 1954. Even in that short space of time things had changed, and initial impressions had to be corrected. When I returned again in 1957–59 I had quite a hard time reconciling some of my earlier findings with what I found then. And on returning to the same part of the same forest yet again in 1970–72, it seemed as though I had to contradict myself all over again. Yet social change has come more slowly and less forcefully to the Ituri than to most parts of Africa. The causes of the changes that had taken place were by no means entirely political or economic, nor did change manifest itself primarily in those spheres of social life. The whole social fabric was permeated by a change that sprang from and was in reaction to a complex multitude of factors. One of those factors, of course, was myself, for in growing older, more experienced, wiser or more foolish, my whole basis for both observation and participation had changed. Even if something was in fact the same (as could be determined by comparing photographs, notes, or third-party accounts) it might well look different to me because *I* had changed.

These are some of the difficulties we have to face in looking at change in any society, but I do not propose to make a detailed comparison of what different people (and the same person) have said at different times about the same phenomenon, and then try to locate the source of disagreement and deduce the cause of change, where that was the source of dissent. That would be a useful exercise, but it is one that anyone can undertake if they are so moved. Since I have been in and out of the Ituri for some thirty years now it seems more profitable to make use of that experience and to concentrate on changes that I have seen taking place within that time span. To start with, I will give a background against which the present situation has to be seen: what we know of the various population movements that led to the relatively recent invasion of the forest by nonforest populations, and so initiated a dramatic change in the form and pace of change in the lives of the indigenous inhabitants.

Then, in Part One, the scene is portrayed as it was in the colonial era, during which time the two populations, hunter-gatherer and farmer-fisher, again had to adapt to a totally new context, modifying the relationship between themselves accordingly. The colonial era ended with independence and the subsequent guerrilla warfare that raged throughout the Ituri for many years, two eyewitness accounts of which are given at the beginning of Part Two, one by a farmer and one by a hunter. Both populations were equally threatened by those years of war, but each emerged in some ways stronger and more unified than before. The years of war had compelled them to come to know each other in a way that had not previously been possible or necessary. But the years of war also created new lines of fission.

I describe what changes I found in 1970, when I returned with a colleague to the Ituri following the years of war. Here we see the process of change continuing, but with an uncertain sense of direction. During this period the now-independent government attempted to induce major reforms and to persuade the hunters to abandon their former way of life, pursued for so many thousands of years with little interference, in order to become sedentary farmers. We still do not know the outcome of this situation, similar to situations faced in many developing nations where segments of the population are barely even aware that the nation exists. But a brief examination of this attempt to accelerate the pace of change for the national good does provide an opportunity to consider what role the anthropologist in the field can or should play.

It is a rare privilege for an anthropologist to be able to return to the field so many times, although it is often disquieting to see some of the changes that have taken place among a people who seem so much at the mercy of the outside world. My own feelings in this respect have changed. But one thing that has not changed is my deep affection for the Mbuti, and although I am constrained by a joking relationship to say nasty things about them occasionally, for the neighboring African village farmers. That affection is mingled with immense respect for the way in which, during those thirty years, they have responded to changes that have taken place all around them, mostly imposed by external forces, without losing their immense zest for life, and without losing their essential humanity, their sense of what is right, meet, and proper, for themselves and for others.

And perhaps this is the place to say, without equivocation, that my affection extends equally and inextricably to the forest itself, for the forest and the people belong together in every respect, even in the eyes of "others." The forest was my first clue to the nature of the people who lived in it. It seemed limitless and totally apart from the rest of the world. Hundreds of miles across in any direction, it seemed almost as vast when one looked upward from the ground, since only in a very few places can the sky be seen through the canopy, which may be more than a hundred feet thick and does not even begin until about fifty feet above the ground. Unlike the world all around it, even at its very edge the forest is cool and shady, in places almost womb-like it seems so protective and all-embracing. It is certainly all-providing to those who know it, offering an abundance of all the necessities of life, and both physical and political security as well. Its very sounds, to the Mbuti, are constant reminders of what they take to be its protective, unquestionably

Even at the edge of the forest there is little direct sunlight, which is diffused as it is reflected downward from leaf to leaf.

benevolent nature. No wonder the songs the Mbuti sing to the forest today are still songs of joy, just as they were when reported in the days of the Pharaohs.

Perhaps that is one of the more important things that we have to learn from any study of change: What kinds of things do people hold onto the most tenaciously, and what aspects of their culture are they most willing to sacrifice when faced with a conscious choice? And even when the choice is not conscious, when social change is more an extended, gradual process of adaptation to an equally gradually changing context, what is it that persists, providing the illusion of continuity, if not of identity with the past? The answer may well be that when a culture persists with little apparent change, as that of the Mbuti seems to have done over a period of many thousands of years, it is not because of a preoccupation with the past, with the maintenance of "tradition," nor even because of a conscious readiness and ability to adapt to the present. Rather, it may be because the people, and the culture, are oriented toward what we would call the future rather than the past, or because both the future and the past are considered by them as relatively insignificant extensions of the ever-changing present.

PART ONE | The Colonial Era

1/General background

"THE MORE IT CHANGES, THE MORE IT IS THE SAME"

It is not possible to say that any human population, at any stage of development, is living in the same way that it was a few hundred, let alone a few thousand years ago. It *is* possible (and profitable) to speculate that whereas no western civilization has remained intact for very long during our paltry history of little more than two thousand years, surviving groups of hunter-gatherers around the world may well have been living in a similar manner, according to similar rules of social behavior and organization, for many thousands of years. Insofar as we respect longevity and survivability, it seems that they have something that we do not.

Yet we plainly have made great achievements in the arts and sciences that few of us would be willing to sacrifice, even in the name of survival. Are the "advances" of civilization incompatible with survival; does civilization, as some believe, comprise a built-in self-destruct system absent in primitive society? If so, then how far is the inherent structural weakness of civilization due to the hard and (virtually) irreversible facts of life today, with its exploding population and rapidly diminishing reservoir of natural resources? Or is it just as much a question of values, which, theoretically at least, *are* reversible?

One of the most dramatic things, for me, that emerges from any study of the Mbuti is their preoccupation with values, and their relative lack of concern with the material world, or, rather, with the world of material well-being. And lest it be said that this is implying that they are somehow more virtuous, or "better" than we are, let me deny that at once. They are whatever they are, like most of us, not because they are better or worse, but because of the context in which they live, and for survival in which they have developed the most satisfactory way of life they could devise. If there is little mendacity and virtually no crime, little attachment to material wealth and great attachment to moral values, it is not because they are "good" or consider these qualities to be virtues, but rather because this is what they *have to be* in order to survive. To lie and steal, to connive and cheat, to amass private wealth, power, and prestige, are simply dysfunctional in their context—or have been up to the present. In societies where they, or similar actions, become essential for survival, they are on their way to becoming accepted modes of behavior, if not virtues.

11

That is the other thing that awakens the romantic in many of us when we take a close look at small-scale societies. Though there may be much that we dislike personally, and certain modes of behavior we could never accept for ourselves, we frequently find that those who have not yet graduated to the level of civilization nonetheless practice many of the virtues extolled as such by civilization, including the ten commandments, rather better than most civilized people. Yet however much, as anthropologists, we come to respect, admire, even love the people we have worked and lived with, I cannot think of any of us who have claimed that we have discovered a society of angels, devoid of human weakness. The Mbuti are certainly as human as any of us, and as individuals as far from perfection, perhaps, as most of us. Yet in terms of human relationships, human consideration, I cannot think of a point in the history of western civilization when we could have claimed to be their equals.

Has it always been so? It is important at least to attempt to answer the question, so that we can know whether this is just another temporary phenomenon or something that has endured and proven itself through time. It is significant that the ancient Egyptians, over four thousand years ago, provide us with an account of pygmies living in the same part of the same forest (near the "mountains of the moon") and characterize them by their abilities as singers and dancers and by their religious devotion to the forest rather than by their remarkably short stature, which gets only incidental mention. This is not much to go on, and although about 500 B.C. Herodotus makes mention of them and their capture of a Nasamonian expedition sent to discover the source of the Nile, Homer accords them almost mythical status. Aristotle refers to their existence in "the land from which flows the Nile," and the Pompeian wall paintings depict pygmies in what could be a contemporary Ituri Forest setting, with the same beehive-shaped huts that are used today. In the sixth century A.D. we get one last isolated reference to pygmies as real people, from an eye-witness report of the Emperor Justinian's ambassador to Ethiopia, who came across "a tribe of pygmies" on an island off the East African coast. But from then on the existence of pygmies is treated as a myth. The fourteenth-century cartographer who drew the famous Hereford Mappa Mundi placed them accurately enough near the alleged source of the Nile, but depicted them as monsters and referred to them (perhaps following Aristotle's lead) as troglodytes. In the seventeenth century an English anatomist, by careful scientific study of skeletal remains, proved that the existence of pygmies was truly a myth, that the creature seen and reported as being a pygmy was in fact a form of chimpanzee. That is not surprising, since the skeleton Tyson examined, which survived until recently, was indeed that of a chimpanzee. Even after some nineteenth-century explorers had reported the factual existence of pygmies, rumors persisted, and into this century we still have published reports of them as flying from treetop to treetop, as having tails, or as crawling on their bellies like snakes to enter their diminutive dwellings.

From such a checkered written history there is little that we can say, except about our own (western) fascination with the idea that there should or could be such a people. But the Pompeian and much earlier Egyptian sources do tell us a couple of important things, namely, that even that far back some pygmies at least were, as they are today, a forest people, and that they considered themselves as such and expressed themselves as such through song and dance.

Forest archaeology has been much neglected because of the limited rewards it has to offer in comparison with archaeology in more arid environments, where material culture has a much better chance of survival. There are clear indications of a very early (Sangoan) population of forest hunters, but we have no way of determining whether or not these were ancestral to the contemporary Mbuti whom we first came to know through the accounts of a Fourth-Dynasty expedition from Egypt. But for the pygmies already to have been established in the forest, as a "people of the trees" and as "dancers of God," that early in recorded history they cannot have been recent arrivals. So we can assume with reasonable certainty that the contemporary Mbuti of the Ituri Forest are descended from pygmy hunter-gatherers who lived in the same forest at the very least five thousand years ago.

To answer the question of how far they or their life-style have changed during that time, we have only the fragile evidence of the Pompeian paintings (and a few mosaics), as well as the Egyptian account. So far as these sources go, they reveal no difference between then and now. But we *can* ask what incentive there might have been for change, and look for evidence of climatic or environmental change, of population movement, or of other factors that might have suggested, made possible, or even demanded change and/or adaptation. Here again we find little or nothing that suggests any reason that there should have been any dramatic change in life-style over this period of time, until the past four or five hundred years perhaps. Further, given the nature of the tropical rain forest as an ecological system, and given the technological possibilities available to the Mbuti, there are not many alternative subsistence patterns they could have followed as long they have been forest dwellers, and that in turn limits the range of possible variation in forms of social organization.

ECONOMIC FACTORS

The equatorial rain forest in Africa, which today stretches from the west coast right across to the Rift Valley and up to the very border of the deserts that lie to the north, predates any population that could have been ancestral to the Mbuti. The glacial changes that brought about fluctuations in the deserts collectively known as the Sahara, parts of which in recorded history were relatively green and fertile, evidently wrought less change on the equatorial forest to the immediate south, though at its fringes it too has been subject to change. What changes the availability of peripheral grazing and browsing might have brought about in the forest fauna and flora is difficult to estimate in detail, yet even a small detail might have had far-reaching consequences in the hunting and gathering technology (hence social organization) of the indigenous forest population. However, many species of contemporary fauna and flora, rather like the Mbuti themselves, seem to be very specifically adaptations to that particular environment, distinct from similar species that are better adapted to the savanna, grassland, and desert lands that surround the forest.

Given the high probability of a lack of significant environmental change over the past five thousand years, and not seeking to push our inquiry back further than that, we can say that the Mbuti have had much the same resources available to them for that period of time, and the same technological possibilities. In fact, whereas the much earlier Sangoan hunters had a stone-age technology, the Mbuti, since we have known of them, have been at a pre-stone-age level, not using any stone implements, and until very recently not making much use of the iron made available to them by immigrant populations.

At this level of technology the Mbuti are limited to a number of cooperative techniques in their exploitation of forest fauna and flora for subsistence. Given the poor visibility of a primary forest, where the canopy of trees meets high overhead, shutting out all direct sunlight, and where the forest floor is interlaced by streams and rivers along which there is dense ground cover that offers ideal refuge for game, individual hunting with spear or bow and arrow is not likely to be very profitable. That is clearly seen today, and underscores the threat of ostracism or banishment, for it is virtually impossible to survive alone in that forest. Yet the forest is full to abundance with edible foods of all kinds, at all times of the year. It is only accessible, however, at the technological level of the Mbuti, through intensive cooperation and/or division of labor.

Yet, although the environmental changes that may have taken place over this period of time are probably infinitesimal, and the range of technological possibilities small, we can be sure that change has taken place, just as it continues to take place today wherever the Mbuti continue to pursue their traditional way of life. For change was an essential ingredient of that way of life, and still is. We shall see when we look at the forest world of the Mbuti in the colonial era (which is when we get our first accurate factual documentation of the Mbuti) that the forest has a rhythm of its own, a waxing and waning that is not precisely seasonal, but does somewhat correspond to fluctuations in a relatively constant rainfall. In response to this rhythm the Mbuti have a rhythm of their own, and exploit the forest's rhythm to their own advantage: social, political, and religious, as well as economic. Thus the size of the hunting bands waxes and wanes throughout each year, relieving tensions almost as soon as they build up, and providing opportunities for a wide-reaching network of interband communication. This makes possible the gathering of relatively large numbers of Mbuti in one place at one time for festive purposes, and equally makes possible the fragmentation of hunting bands into tiny units that can manifest their social solidarity with even greater intensity—the lineal family as distinct from the larger "economic family," which is how the hunting band might be described.

Thus from one camp to the next (and they move every month) there is change, and the change is nearly always an adaptive response either to the rhythm of the forest and the potential for subsistence it offers the Mbuti, or to the political or social needs of the Mbuti themselves. Accompanying such changes there is also a subtle shift in religious values. However slight, the change is *total* in that it affects *all* areas of social life.

DEMOGRAPHIC FACTORS

It is difficult, given the facts we have about the primary forest as an ecosystem, to see that life can have been much different however far back into the past we can reach, as long as we remain within the confines of the forest. It is only in recent times, due to the immigration of alien, nonforest populations, that the pace of social change has accelerated, and its nature significantly altered. That is, it has changed from being a nondirectional, sensitive response to the rhythms of the forest to being a less sensitive, more urgent, and unidirectional response (which we refer to as progress, advance, or evolution) to other cultures, technologically dominant and with totally different value systems. At first these other populations were African farmers and cattle herders forced reluctantly into the (for them) hostile forest by the population explosion that began about two thousand years ago, but did not reach the Ituri until the past few hundred years. Then came the Arab slave trade, and hard on its heels that almost equally disastrous phenomenon known as Henry Morton Stanley, who effectively opened the Congo to colonial exploitation.

Following the colonial era, which induced more change in a decade than the forest had seen in its living history, there was the post-independence era, a decade of internecine guerrilla warfare that ravaged the Ituri and its population. And even when that was over, the Mbuti found themselves subject to still different forces of change. These emanated from the African government of the new nation of Zaïre, which called on the Mbuti to leave the forest and their hunting-gathering way of life and become sedentary farmers, or enter national service, or find other more "productive" occupations and thus make their economic and political contribution to the new nation. Even up to that point, and I was there when it happened, the Mbuti had little or no concept of what a nation was, or of where the capital of their particular nation lay, or of who made up the government, except that like their representatives, who sometimes ventured along the roadside that cuts through the middle of the forest, they were all foreigners, as foreign as the colonials had been, as foreign as the slave traders, as foreign as anyone who was not a forest person. From this ancient and singularly "egocentric" point of view the Mbuti were in a poor position to deal with the changes forced upon them.

Here we are dealing with a kind of change completely different from the rhythmic monthly adaptive changes that mark the traditional way of life of the Mbuti. The traditional dynamic change that characterizes their hunting-gathering way of life never departs far from a central but undefined focal point. It is concentric, or even centripetal, whereas the kind of change that faces the Mbuti today was at first eccentric, then centrifugal, if not helical. We shall have to return to this point later; the important thing here is to show that even though "change" may be nothing new to the Mbuti, the kind of change to which they have been accustomed in no way prepares them for the change they are facing today. If anything, it places them at an even greater disadvantage. After all, when a centrifuge is started the various parts attached to the circumference seem to revolve around a common center, at least, though not tending towards it, as in centripetal motion. But from the very outset of foreign influence the tendency has been increasingly to fly away from the center, and this would indeed happen if there were not some adequately strong retaining bond. When such a bond breaks, then the peripheral part will fly off, perhaps in a straight line with no further regard for the old center of attachment, or if some attractive force proves strong enough, in a kind of helical movement, still related to the old central point, but getting ever further away, with no possibility of return.

It is essential to keep in mind the qualitative difference between different kinds of change, the essential difference between change that transforms, altering the outer and/or inner nature of the subject, and the change that adapts or modifies, retaining the essential character of the subject. We also have to consider the enormous difference between change that comes about by the process of evolution, or gradual development, and that which comes about by mutation or imposition: sudden, dramatic, unpredictable.

FAUNA AND FLORA

Returning now to a consideration of the forest itself and the many thousands of years during which all evidence suggests that the Mbuti lived there without any trace of influence from the outside, nonforest world, we can assert that although the Mbuti were well accustomed to change, it was either "concentric" or "centripetal." That is, it was always directly related to and centered around the forest itself, if not some particular part of the forest. What we cannot know, at the moment, is what changes occurred as the hunter-gatherers moved from one part of the forest to another; we do not even know if such movement took place, or if it did whether it was easterly or westerly. The importance of this is that while the tropical rain forest, particularly where it is equatorial (as it is in the case of the Ituri) is in many respects uniform throughout, there are subtle but significant variations in fauna and flora. My own early impressions of the Ituri were of variations in altitude and consequently of terrain, the eastern part of the forest being much more mountainous than the central and western area. I did not notice any significant difference in either the fauna or flora, however, either through direct observation or through examination of the material culture of the Mbuti. There was nonetheless a dramatic difference in the hunting techniques of the Mbuti in different parts of the forest. To the east, in the more mountainous region, they were archers, hunting primarily with bow and arrow. To the west and in the central region they used nets. In the north there was a much smaller Mbuti population that seemed primarily to use spears.

Recent studies made by a highly specialized team of Japanese anthropologists point to the fact that this difference in hunting technique may be related to certain changes in the flora. Most significantly, the smaller trees, shrubs, and undergrowth vary in height and density, just as the soil varies, and one crucial form of vegetation, known locally as *nkusa* is more abundant in just that part of the forest where we find the net-hunters, whose nets are made from *nkusa* (Tanno 1976,

103). This is yet another example of how intimately the life of the Mbuti, even their hunting technology, is related to the ecosystem of which they are a part—a dynamic relationship we do not yet fully understand. Even a slight movement of population, then, could either deprive a population of certain hunting possibilities or make a new technology available.

It is perhaps more possible that nets were introduced when Bantu-speaking populations invaded the forest, bringing their own technology with them. We cannot be sure. But whether induced by indigenous population movement or by diffusion from an immigrant population, there resulted a considerable change in the overall social organization, clearly differentiating the archers from the net hunters in more ways than mere hunting technology. Yet the intriguing thing is that despite this disparity the sense of unity, even identity, is unaffected. It is almost as though both groups consciously work at maintaining an underlying unity. Each accepts the constraints imposed upon them by the environment and their technology, but modifies their hunting technique, taking advantage of whatever latitude the forest allows them, so as to recreate an observable similarity of life-style that overshadows the obvious dissimilarity of hunting technique. It is always dangerous to impute motives. I mention this "impression" of conscious manipulation, however, because the Mbuti themselves minimize the difference and maximize the similarities.

With regard to the forest fauna we are not so well informed. The same group of Japanese anthropologists did some admirable work on fauna and on game consumption (Harako 1976, Ichikawa 1978, Tanno 1976), but we still know far too little about the distribution of game, and still less about the movement of game, migratory patterns, and so forth. Perhaps the Harvard expedition in the field at this moment will bring information back, before the patterns of game movement are too drastically changed by the continued and ever-increasing exploitation of the forest.

However, any changes that might have taken place in the past involving the fauna must have led to corresponding changes, not just in hunting technology, but very likely in all other aspects of social organization, including religious belief. When I was first among the Mbuti, in 1951, the hunting territories that divided the forest, extending from the periphery in towards the center, never met at the center. There the Mbuti left an inner circle surrounding a "no man's land" in which all hunting was prohibited. Any game that escaped from the hunt and made its way into that circle was not pursued. It has been suggested (Van Gelder, Mammalogy Department, American Museum of Natural History, personal communication) that this custom functioned primarily to provide a sanctuary for any species that were in danger of being overhunted. The institutionalized prohibition on hunting in this area was supported by religious belief.

In fact, it is in their system of religious belief and practice that the Mbuti demonstrate the comprehensiveness of their adaptation to the forest world and their role as an effective part of the forest ecosystem. They have few myths of the past, but one myth of origin does suggest that once they lived exclusively as gatherers, in total harmony with the forest. Then, according to that myth, one day an Mbuti killed an animal, and to conceal the crime consumed it, turning to practical use every part that he could not eat. Since that day, say the Mbuti, all animals (including humans) have been condemned to die. Until then they were immortal, like the forest itself. The forest (flora) continues to be immortal. Only the Mbuti can restore immortality to the animal kingdom, by finding a way to survive without hunting. Yet from that moment of original sin they have been condemned to be hunters, perpetuating their mortality. This, of course, is a magnificent argument for game conservation, and in the view of mammalogists such as Van Gelder the hunters are indeed the finest conservationists any conservation-minded government could wish for.

This has profound implications when we come to consider the situation today, where one of the changes wrought by an increase in the immigrant population is an increase in the demand that the Mbuti hunt for more than they need for themselves, spending more and more time hunting. In the past, even up to the independence of Zaire, their religious beliefs influenced the Mbuti to hunt only when they had no food for that day. This resulted in hunting only about five days each week, and for only about four hours each day. Any change that compels the Mbuti to increase their hunting activities will, as they see it, increase their mortality—a powerful incentive to resist such change, we might think.

The forest fauna are incorporated into the Mbuti social organization in many other ways, as symbols, as a source of material for making various artifacts or forms of body ornamentation, and as indicators of climatic change. Again, it seems that the Mbuti almost consciously work at heightening this already intensive and highly practical interaction. For instance, they insist that it is the cry of the chameleon that tells them when honey is ready, in the "honey season." This is a very distinctive, long-drawn-out, high-pitched, flute-like sound, almost like a deep-toned whistle. It can be heard most often at night, and, sure enough, when the Mbuti go off in that direction the next day they will return with honey. However, I have been informed by highly qualified specialists that the chameleon is incapable of making any such sound, and I am also highly suspicious about the Mbuti assertion concerning a "honey season" restricted to about two months (May-July) of the year, for I have found honey at almost all times of the year. Others assert that this is so, that it is merely more abundant at that particular time of year. As we shall see when we look at the hunting techniques of both archers and net hunters, it is essential for them to have an annual occasion on which they come together or split up, respectively, for political purposes. In the absence of noticeable and predictable seasonal variation, could it be that the Mbuti invented "a honey season" for just such a function?

I would not put it past them, yet as a footnote I have to report that in Uganda a botanist recorded the same long, drawn-out, whistling, flute-like cry in the Budongo Forest, and was told that it was the cry of the chameleon. And it has been reported from as far away as Sri Lanka that the Veddas, the native forest people there, associate the cry of the chameleon with honey.

Whatever the truth of the matter, the fact that concerns us here is the consciousness among the Mbuti of their functional interdependence with the forest world. For understanding the implications of change, induced or otherwise, clear recognition of this interdependence, be it real or imagined, is essential.

Whatever changes in social organization occurred during movement of the Mbuti from one part of the forest to another, or through any of the minor climatic alterations that may have affected the Ituri fauna and flora during the past five thousand years, were probably minimal. (That is, changes other than the change from gathering to a combination of this with hunting, and the diversification between hunting with bow and arrow and hunting with net.) Such changes were, in addition, likely to have been gradual, essentially adaptive developments, and concentric or centripetal in nature. It is when we come to consider the invasion of nonforest populations, mostly farmers from the neighboring grasslands and savanna, that we find the nature of change changing in pace and character. Even then, what we notice most among the Mbuti is the way that they adapt so as to preserve their integrity, as they see it, as *bamiki bandura*, literally "children of the forest."

TECHNOLOGICAL INNOVATION

The population explosion that took place among the west-coast agriculturalists spread through the forest to the south, along the savanna fringe to the north of the forest, and, only reluctantly and more slowly, right through the forest itself, eastwards, until it reached the Ituri. Estimates vary, but it seems that it was between three and five hundred years ago that the Ituri first began to be exploited by an immigrant population. As farmers, they brought new technologies with them, new world views, different concepts of time and space, and entirely different social systems. Bantu-speaking peoples invaded the forest from east, south, and west, while Sudanic speakers came from the north. They brought with them concepts of empire, nation, chiefdom, and tribe, all alien political forms to the forest hunters, loosely organized as they were into loosely interconnected but otherwise independent bands of no more than a few families each in size.

More significantly, for the Mbuti, the intruders brought new weapons and tools. The powerful but clumsy cross-bow stopped at the Ubangi River, though even there the pygmy hunters seem to have rejected it as more destructive than helpful. Its use in that part of the rain forest is confined mainly to the immigrant populations who brought it with them. But in the Ituri the immigrants brought spears and bows and arrows that were significantly different from those used by the Mbuti. They were bigger, more powerful, and above all, both spears and arrows were tipped with iron blades. These were made readily available to the Mbuti through trade, but even into the colonial era they remained largely trade items as far as the Mbuti were concerned; they continued to prefer their fire-hardened wooden spear and arrow tips, tips they impregnated with poison. The major use that the Mbuti found for this new material, metal, was as blades for knives, as machettes for cutting the saplings with which they build their house frames, and as tiny axe blades that helped them to enlarge the hole around where bees had nested in a tree bole, making it easier to extract the honey.

None of these iron tools were *necessary*, but they were convenient. Even on my last visit (1970–72) after independence I saw bamboo being used as a cutting utensil, and digging sticks used to extract honey. As a weapon only the spear blade truly found favor, and that particularly for use in the hunting of elephant by what seems to have been a recently introduced technique of hobbling the animal by slashing the heel tendons. Yet I have known Mbuti to still go off in what they claim to be the old manner, with fire-hardened spear points well impregnated with poison, and kill an elephant by running beneath the beast and thrusting the spear through the abdomen into the bladder. The wound does not kill the animal, but it will die of peritonitis, usually within twenty-four hours.

The newly available iron technology opened up other possibilities for improving the daily catch of game; for instance, tools were now available for the digging of pit traps, something many villagers do to protect the plantations around their homes. But the Mbuti seem to have consciously rejected any such "improvement," and later they consciously rejected the use of guns, which could have enabled them to kill even greater quantities of game, giving them an enormous economic advantage over the protein-starved village farmers. It was plain that as far as the Mbuti were concerned the quality of life was more important to them than the quantitative element of individual wealth, which was the lure held out to them by those who wished to change them for their own purposes. The primary economic standard of the Mbuti seems to have been one of "adequacy." Inadequacy was unknown (the Mbuti say that "the only hungry Mbuti is a lazy Mbuti"). The forest is well enough stocked with edible flora and fauna to support a much larger population. Surplus was, as already described, consciously avoided, as a mortal sin. The necessarily nomadic style of life militates against the acquisition of private property, and the necessarily cooperative food-getting techniques stress the social good as against the individual good.

Several forms of adaptation could have taken place when the Mbuti found themselves suddenly surrounded by nonforest farmers, whose survival depended on claiming territory for themselves, fighting other immigrant peoples, if necessary, to establish such claims. The contact between the two peoples could have led to warfare, for it must have seemed that the two ways of life were mutually exclusive: Whereas the Mbuti depend for their survival on keeping the forest untouched, the immigrants, for *their* survival, as farmers, depended on cutting the forest down. But the only fighting was among the immigrants themselves as they competed for territory around the periphery of the forest, fighting in which the Mbuti served as guides, spies, and scouts. As such, they were, of course, in an ideal position to keep the warring immigrants confined to the edges of the forest, which to a large extent they did. However, they *could* have fought, and with their intimate knowledge of the forest, even given their lack of central political organization, might well have won.

But they did not fight. Nor did they seize the opportunity offered them to become assimilated, or simply by imitation to change from hunting to farming and to pursue the quest for individual power, prestige, and wealth. Nor did they relocate to avoid contact, an alternative that was open to them at least for a time. And, finally, they made no attempt to convert the newcomers to their way of thinking, to make hunters, forest people, of them.

Again the Mbuti exhibited a remarkable unity for such a loosely organized, politically uncentralized population. Whether dealing with the Sudanic speakers to the north and east, or the Bantu-speaking farmers elsewhere, whether dealing with empires and kingdoms like those of the Zande and Mangbetu, or petty chiefdoms and tribes like those of the Bira and Ndaka, the Mbuti uniformly retained the integrity of their forest way of life. At the same time they encouraged the immigrants to maintain *their* own life-styles and values.

The cost was what has often been mistaken for servitude, or subordination at least. In fact, the Mbuti merely provided a few services that they could well afford to do, without unduly interfering with their traditional way of life. In particular, they provided the villagers with certain essential resources from the interior of the forest: saplings and leaves for house-building, bark for cloth-making, salt, and, above all, meat for protein. The gain, from the Mbuti point of view, was incomparable. What they secured in this manner was the exclusion of the farmers from the inner forest. They confined the bulk of them to the periphery, allowing only a few immigrants to push in along the major waterways that cut through the forest. Thus the Mbuti hunting and gathering territory was retained intact, unthreatened by the destructive slash-and-burn techniques of the farmers, who instead shifted around at the edge of the forest, where they could do it little harm, yet where they could have a perfectly adequate living of their own, in their own preferred manner.

One of the more significant changes that took place during this time had to do with language. Each population retained its own subsistence activity, though the immigrants had to adapt to a very new environment. Each retained its own form of political organization, though again the immigrants had to adapt, particularly those who scattered as they pushed inwards along the waterways. Each retained its own system of religious beliefs, the immigrants again adapting to take account of the new world in which they had come to live. As far as we can tell, each retained its own system of domestic organization, including the kinship system, though here it may be that the Mbuti had to do the most adapting, for political reasons. The biggest change of all was that which came to the Mbuti, who, it seems, lost their own language and adopted those of the immigrant peoples with whom they had contact. Only by virtue of the fact that most Mbuti speak several languages can an Mbuti from one side of the forest now communicate with one from the other side of the forest, since most of the languages introduced are mutually unintelligible, some being Sudanic and some being Bantu. The process by which the Mbuti lost their language is not much to be wondered at, fragmented as they were into isolated hunting bands, each band a "minority" in the context of the village world to which it attached itself, however temporarily. But again, what strikes us is that even in adopting the languages of the newcomers, the Mbuti largely rejected the concepts that came with the languages. To this day they use those languages in a way that makes them all but incomprehensible to their original speakers.

Thus early investigators had the impression that the Mbuti were not only subservient, for they provided economic help without any apparent economic return or payment, but also grossly acculturated, for they spoke the language, in each tribal area, of "their masters." This appearance was heightened by the fact that when they came out of the forest to visit or work in a village, the Mbuti behaved in most respects like villagers, if somewhat unruly villagers. They aped the village customs, used the same technology, subordinated themselves to the village political system (under which they had little status), and attached themselves to family households, using the village system of kinship terminology, as though they were junior members of the family. These relationships persisted through time, giving the appearance of inherited serfdom, if not slavery. As we shall see, this is far from the truth, but the image persists, and the confusion resulting from differential usage of the same languages and the same kinship terminology makes it extremely difficult to make a true assessment of what is truly the "Mbuti" system. It seems to be one thing in the forest, and another when they are in the village.

INVASION AND AGGRESSION

Both Mbuti and villagers refer to these early years of contact as years of war, but by this term the villagers primarily refer to the years that followed, when the Arab slave traders moved in from the east in quest of ivory and of slaves to carry the ivory back to the coast, where both could be sold together. The Ituri today is bisected by a dirt road that largely follows the old slave trail, which can still be seen where the two part company, for the trail was blazed by cutting down the primary vegetation and is easily recognized wherever you see an avenue of secondary vegetation.

These "years of war" were intensified by yet another war, one which was still remembered by old men and women I met when I first visited the Ituri in 1951. It was the "Bula Matari War," the war that was Stanley—Stanley when he fought his way through to find the source of the great Congo River, and above all Stanley when he rampaged and ravished his way through the Ituri Forest, no less than three times back and forth, on his expedition to relieve Emin Pasha. The cost in human life and suffering is incalculable. It was overlooked and quickly forgotten in Europe, because the cost was mainly in African lives and African suffering. But it was not forgotten in the Ituri, where, in the fifties, the senseless slaughter, the indignities, the public "executions" were still within living memory.

And it lives on today in legend; but it is a legend told primarily by villagers, while Mbuti recount the legend of the earlier years of war, when they cunningly kept the invading villagers from entering and ravaging their domain. Stanley's brutal expeditions had little impact on the Mbuti, except perhaps to warn them, as it warned others, what they might expect from other Europeans. Even slavery only touched them in so far as they were encouraged to kill elephants in order to provide the Arabs with the ivory. This undoubtedly had some effect on religious practice, but that is difficult to disentangle. (It involves, among other things, a musicological comparison of elephant-hunting songs, said to be specific to the heel-slashing technique introduced during this time, with the sacred molimo "death" songs.) Suffice it to say here that even the double cataclysm of Henry Morton Stanley and the Arab slave traders (the most notorious of whom Stanley had installed as the first Governor of the eastern province, under Belgian patronage) effected little change (in the sense of transformation) among the Mbuti. Again, the hunters merely made the minimal adaptations necessary to maintain their chosen way of life as intact as possible.

Even under the colonial rule of the Belgians the Mbuti continued to adapt rather than change, but during that era new forces were at work that foreshadowed what is probably the end of one of the longest-lived and most successful human experiments known. The Mbuti genius for adaptation seems to have met its match. The demands of contemporary economics and politics, aided and abetted by modern technology, threatens to transform, if not destroy, the forest, and with it the quality of *forestness*, which is the quality of being an Mbuti. The change that confronts the Mbuti today is centrifugal, tearing them away from the forest, to which they remain attached only, or mainly, by the increasingly tenuous ties of their ideology, rather than by their economy or their role in the overall ecology. And as their forest-oriented values weaken under the strain, they will be flung outwards, never to return. Some, however, and I suspect many, will, in the way of all Mbuti, take a helical course on their outward-bound journey, spiraling away from the forest rather than flying off at a tangent. This suggests that if only they could tumble off the edge, inwards, they would be drawn back down into the vortex, to be united again with the forest core. If that supposition, or wish, seems un-anthropological, at least it follows Mbuti imagery in supposing that if only they could learn how to survive without the violence of killing other animals, they might retain their immortality.

2/The forest world

THE TWO POPULATIONS

When I first visited the Ituri Forest, in 1951, it was as though the colonial era had hardly touched it. I entered the forest from Uganda, following a barely passable mud road pitted by potholes the size of small craters, some big enough to engulf an entire truck. The rolling, open grasslands give way abruptly to primary forest. Coming down to the Ituri River itself, for instance, you are in open grassland on one side of the river and on the far side you can see a huge black wall of trees approaching two hundred feet in height, rising sheer from the very edge of the water. In those days all but the smallest rivers had to be crossed by ferry, adding to the sense of isolation, and providing yet another hazard and source of delay for motor transport of any kind.

The road through the forest was in even worse condition, since for most of its course the trees met high overhead, preventing the sunlight from drying out the surface, which was drenched by torrential downpours almost every day. On either side of this narrow road the forest presented a seemingly impenetrable wall, as solid and forbidding as along the river banks. For five or ten miles at a stretch there might be no sign of life other than the occasional massive, steaming droppings of an elephant that had crossed the road, or a troop of baboons that would disappear at the very last moment, a few of the boldest peering out from the thick foliage. But if you stopped and listened the forest seemed to be bursting with life, albeit invisible.

The only place the road widened and the trees thinned out was when approaching a village of the immigrant farmers. These were rectangular villages with the road running through the middle. In the old days (and still in remote parts where the villages are connected only by foot trail) each end of the village used to be closed by a guard house, and many were stockaded. Each was surrounded by a small area of forest cleared for the villagers' plantations of manioc, plantains, dry rice, peanuts, and perhaps some corn and beans. The village itself was thus in the middle of a tiny enclave of sunlight, surrounded by an immense wall of forest. Not only were the villages isolated from each other by many miles, they seemed isolated from and insulated against the forest itself. They were mostly hot and dusty. The rectangular mud houses were thatched with leaves lashed down with long saplings and were grouped in little clusters, each cluster marked by an open sitting place,

24

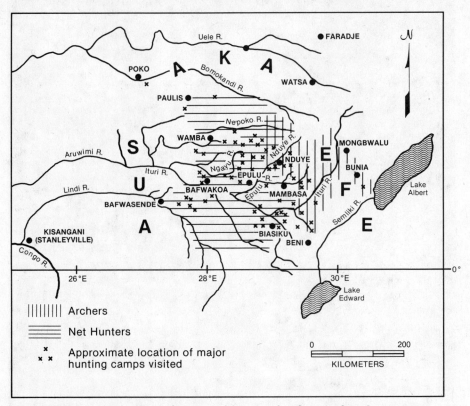

Map 3: Approximate location of hunting bands visited in the Ituri.

or *baraza*, shaded by a roof of the same phrynium leaves. For most of the day the villages seemed as deserted as the road. Even the *barazas* were empty until late afternoon.

Further into the forest, some of the villages, particularly among the Ndaka (who were fishermen rather than farmers), seemed less self-consciously buttressed against the forest around them. Some let trees grow in the middle of the village, sheltering the rooftops at least to some extent from the hot equatorial sun. The Ndaka seemed more in tune with their world, decorating the walls of their houses with painted geometric designs. But even those villages had a feeling of impermanence about them, as though the huge forest that hugged the very walls of some of the houses was waiting to engulf the entire population.

Very rarely a small party of Mbuti pygmies might be seen along the roadside, but in those days they disappeared at first sight. Today they would be more likely to call out to others to join them and accost the unwary traveler, thumbing a ride or trying for a handout with the assurance of any panhandler The latter development, however, might best be considered as adaptation rather than change, as we shall see. In the depths of the forest those selfsame Mbuti who are so mercenary along the roadside, willing to sell almost anything for a pittance, are little changed

In colonial days the road running through the heart of the forest was in most places barely wide enough to allow two vehicles to pass and was shaded in most places from direct sunlight. Today it is an open, arid, and dusty highway (compare photo page 99).

from what they were when I first knew them, running to hide from any foreigner who passed. Then, as now, they kept the two worlds apart, and spent the least amount of time possible anywhere near the road.

And how different their forest world was. Far from being impenetrable, once the tangle of secondary growth has been passed the forest opens out into a cool, green wonderland where you can walk with ease, comfort, and safety. The leafy canopy high overhead protects you from the heat and glare of direct sunlight, and

If villages are not constantly tended they quickly become overgrown, which adds to the hostility and mistrust the villagers feel toward the world around them.

the leaves and twigs underfoot protect you against snakes and any predators that might be sleeping nearby, warning them well in advance of your approach. The Mbuti reinforce this protection by shouting and singing as they go through the forest. Just about the only animal that might attack unprovoked is the forest buffalo, and even it will not attack if there is too much noise.

This is the world of the Mbuti, a world from which they had managed to exclude the immigrant village farmers and fishers, keeping them confined to their little enclaves around the periphery of what, for the Mbuti, was the *real* world, of *real* people and *real* animals and *real* vegetation. They found the villagers as strange in appearance and as clumsy as their domesticated animals, and their cultivated plants as puny and insignificant as they were unnecessary in a forest that offered real people everything they needed, just for the taking. In this natural refuge the Mbuti had until then escaped and held back not only the successive waves of immigrants that threatened to penetrate the forest from all sides, but also the slave traders, and even the Belgian colonials. Their daily round of hunting and gathering, and their pattern of moving their hunting camps every month, following wherever the forest beckoned, was undisturbed.

Even the village world was relatively little affected by the European presence. The road that ran through the center of the forest was little more than a consolidation of the old slave trail that was used by Stanley on his marches backward and forward between the Uganda border and the Congo River. Other than a little gold at the eastern edge of the forest, there was little of economic importance to the Belgians in the Ituri. Transportation problems (some fifteen hundred miles to the coast) made its exploitation for lumber totally impractical, and it was little more than a pious hope that some enterprising Belgian planters might be able to develop forest land for coffee, and perhaps cotton, thus adding at least something to the colonial coffers from an otherwise unproductive region. As a result, not much money was invested in the administration of the region. The road was not completed until the thirties (and to this day is barely motorable, and at times totally impassable). And though the government appointed its own chosen "chiefs" to replace the more powerful traditional rulers, they tended to leave the village farmers alone provided they did not fight, too openly at least, and paid their taxes.

To a certain extent the imposition of taxes and the demand that the village farmers grow cotton indirectly affected the Mbuti, whom the administration totally ignored for all practical purposes. Yet Putnam, an American anthropologist who had already been in the Ituri for a quarter of a century, and others who had spent as long or longer in the same general area all reported to the same effect: the colonial era had relatively little impact on the village farmers, and virtually none on the Mbuti. But what impact there was constituted a beginning, and that was all that was needed. The seeds were sown, and both the scope and pace of change began increasing.

The Ituri Forest, depending on how you measure it, is about fifty thousand square miles, and is part of what used to be a much larger forest extending right through to the Atlantic coast, an expanse now broken by large tracts of open farmland. Within the Ituri lived about forty thousand Mbuti pygmies, living much as they had always lived, by hunting and gathering, with a pre-stone-age technology. Mainly around the periphery, but also in a broken line stretching along the old slave trail in the south, lived about the same number of immigrant farmers, who depended on the Mbuti for forest supplies of clothing and building materials and, most of all, for meat. Few of these villagers ever ventured into the forest (and those that did were mainly ritual specialists or outcasts). The movement of these shifting agriculturalists was lateral rather than inward, thus preserving the ecological integrity of the inner forest.

The forest itself was divided into hunting territories, each occupied by a band of Mbuti that was attached (in a manner to be described in the next section) to the village at the periphery. All hunting territories extended inwards, away from the village, to the central region that I have already described as a "no man's land." Fig. 1 represents, in a grossly simplified form, this arrangement, and indicates only some of the major tribal divisions as they stretch around the periphery. However, although I talk of "periphery," and of the villagers as "nonforest" people living "outside" the forest, this is all strictly from an Mbuti point of view. Only to some extent does it correspond to that of the villagers. In fact, the forest continues to stretch beyond the area under discussion here, particularly towards the south, where, indeed, more Mbuti are to be found, though not many. The circle, as drawn, also leaves out of consideration the Mbuti of the southeast, who relate to villages established along the roads that form a triangle connecting Kommanda, Beni, and Mambasa (see Map 2).

An important feature of the diagram in Fig. 1 is that it shows how the central and western Mbuti were disposed with relation to each other and to the peripheral

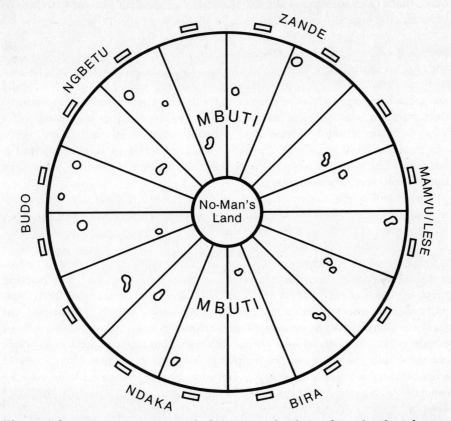

Fig. 1: Schematic representation of the territorial relationship of Mbuti hunters to village farmers. The number of tribal and hunting territories, and of villages and hunting camps, has been considerably reduced. In the center is a "no man's land" in which no hunting takes place, so that it effectively acts as a game sanctuary.

villages. The northern and eastern Mbuti, because of the greater exploitation of that part of the forest (mines, missions, coffee plantations, and administrative posts) seemed to fall into a number of much smaller such circular arrangements.

The diagram also shows how each hunting territory could be identified, even named, for the village at its outer edge. Each village considered that it had "its own hunting territory." To some extent that was true. What was not so true was the assumption by each village that it also owned, or controlled, its own hunting *band*. That is, it claimed that a hereditary relationship existed between its own patrilineal members and the (presumably) patrilineal band that (equally presumably) hunted that territory.

But the diagram shows that each band was not only adjacent to one on the right and one on the left, but through the "no man's land" was effectively adjacent to *all* other bands. The orientation of the Mbuti towards each other and towards the villagers was totally different from that of the villagers toward them. And each month, as the year went by and as bands grew larger and smaller, the composition of each band changed. If, in fact, any one village wanted to bring "its band" out of the forest, it would only find some of those Mbuti, often as few as forty percent of those they claimed, in "their" territory at that moment. The band that would theoretically emerge, at the bidding of the villagers, might consist of as many as sixty members who belonged to other territories, according to the villagers, for every forty they claimed as their own. A total population of one hundred, adults *and* children, would actually be the size of a fairly sizeable band, particularly if it was inhabiting a single hunting camp rather than being divided up within the territory into several hunting camps.

A good look at the diagram makes it clear how easily the Mbuti who are hunting within any one territory can have access to the Mbuti within any other territory, even right across the forest if they so chose. This mobility is of great importance for the Mbuti, as much in their economic life as in their domestic and political life. In theory each territory has equal access to all others, through the central zone (which is only three or four days march from the periphery at any point). For practical purposes, however, mobility is restricted by linguistic considerations, and inter-territorial movement generally follows the connections forged by marriage. For various reasons, also to be discussed later, this means that any one Mbuti, male or female, is likely to confine his or her movements within forest to the area in which one tribal unit holds sway at the periphery, for marriage is most likely to occur within that tribal territory. Few Mbuti, however, are likely to have no kin who are attached to and reside in other tribal territories, and since a claim of kinship is sufficient to grant at least temporary admission to any hunting band, every Mbuti has a wide choice of bands and territories that he or she can join at will, at any time.

The reason we keep deferring discussion of village-related factors is that we will deal with them in the next section. The fact that so far we have had to make constant reference to them shows that the two worlds are inextricably bound together. But by dividing the exposition in this way, and first discussing the forest world as though it were isolated from the nonforest world, I am following another level of reality. One of the remarkable things about the Mbuti is that they seem to be the healthiest schizophrenics in the world. They see themselves in the forest as one thing, and in the village as something else. Their manner of speech and behavior are correspondingly different; they follow different customs, even (apparently) in such vital areas as marriage and mortuary ceremonies, and initiation into adulthood.

The complexity of the forest-village relationship will emerge as we go along, but for the moment let us look at the life of the Mbuti as they lived it in the forest when I was first there, and on one occasion I was with them in successive hunting camps for six months without our ever coming to the peripheral village. During this time we subsisted perfectly well entirely on forest foods, despite the fact that village foods (particularly plantains and manioc) are well liked and eaten in great quantity whenever a band is near the village.

NOMADISM AND MOBILITY

On leaving a village it took under an hour's walk to be in the primary forest. This was true in whatever part of the forest I visited, and I made a survey around the total periphery. Most Mbuti would not establish a hunting camp that close to the village, but it happened often enough. The one advantage was that the village plantations remained within easy reach for raiding purposes, and from such peripheral hunting camps sorties to the villagers' plantations were continually being made by young and old, male and female, individuals and small groups returning with baskets filled with village foodstuffs that had been begged or simply stolen. It was considered as another form of "hunting." Such camps were fun because of the wild stories, mostly terribly exaggerated, of the various tricks and guiles used by the Mbuti to cheat the "stupid" villagers, and again the hunting metaphor was used. Mbuti are great mimes, and the whole band would gather around to watch as the various stories of theft and deceit and trickery were acted out.

What made it all the more hilarious is that the village was only an hour or so away, almost within earshot. Yet we knew we were totally immune, since no villager would have dared venture that far into the forest, even in pursuit of stolen goods. It was an almost universal belief among all villagers, regardless of tribal affiliation, that the forest was filled with dangerous and malevolent spirits, to whom the Mbuti were closely allied. As a matter of fact, it was the Mbuti themselves who were largely responsible for these beliefs, always telling the villagers about the grotesque monsters that even they had to contend with in the forest. It was one of their many techniques for making sure that the villagers stayed outside the forest world.

But soon there would be a subtle change of mood. The appetite for village delicacies and for the fun of tricking and ridiculing the villagers would wane, and we would all feel an urge to move on. Then one morning, soon after light began to filter through the leafy canopy nearly two hundred feet overhead, men were busy rolling up their hunting nets and women were packing their few belongings into the large baskets they carried on their backs, held in place by tump lines running across their foreheads. Mothers also carried their youngest children, up to three years old, on one hip. Older children carried a few other household possessions, or other children. The male youths armed themselves with bows and arrows, while the married men, carrying the nets, held spears at the ready. The elders carried little or nothing; like anyone who was sick or crippled, they had all their needs taken care of and just made their own way in their own time.

Some village foods need special cooking utensils. Rice has to be boiled, so either metal or earthen cooking pots are needed. The Mbuti have none of these, so they too have to be begged or stolen. Plantains and manioc can be roasted in hot coals, but some prefer them boiled, or pounded to a pulp in a heavy wooden mortar, which similarly has to be filched from the village. When we were proceeding further into the forest I was always astounded at how many of these utensils would be left behind. But it was pointed out to me that, for one thing, they were too heavy to carry far, and, for another, they were not needed for cooking the forest foods on which we would live in the deep forest. Anyway, the hunters could always hunt for more pots and mortars whenever they wanted them, they said, breaking yet again into a comic pantomime showing how easily the stupid villagers were fooled.

Yet with all this mockery and ridicule, and very real trickery, there was never a trace of malice or real hostility. If anything, it was really rather friendly ridicule, a form of group joking relationship that merely helped to establish the clear and necessary difference between "them" and "us." Simple preference marked the essential difference, rather than any sense of superiority or inferiority.

As it happened, I loved the cool and dim light of the forest and the high humidity did not bother me at all; it was much less oppressive than the heat and dust of the village. And whereas the water in the villages tended to be contaminated enough to give me stomach disorders, I could drink from any forest stream with impunity. Above all, in the forest there were no mosquitos or flies, except high up in the canopy or along the banks of the wider rivers. My obvious pleasure in being away from the village, and the fact that, through stupidity rather than bravery, I was totally unafraid, quickly classified me as a "forest person" rather than a "villager."

That was fine by me, but it plainly colored my field work, giving me much greater access to the lives and thoughts and dreams of the Mbuti than I could otherwise ever have had, but at the same time denying me equal access to the world of the villagers, who came to regard me with the same kind of rather amused disdain that they had, or pretended to have, for the Mbuti. Once, proud of having learned one of their languages (KiBira) from the Mbuti, I tried it out in a Bira village. But they said (somewhat contemptuously) they had a hard time understanding me because I spoke "just like an Mbuti." To some extent I was always excluded from the inner world of the villagers. But then, any fieldworker is limited by many things—by his or her gender, age, marital status, food preferences, stamina, and health. The best we can do is to accept those limitations knowingly, take whatever corrective action is possible, and not pretend to omniscience.

During all those first three field trips, during the colonial era, I fell into the same role as a classificatory Mbuti, and spent my time with them whether they were in village or forest. They seldom stayed in the village for more than a few days at any one time, and the deeper they went into the forest the longer they stayed away, though in the Epulu region, where I mostly worked, the village was never more than a fast three-days walk away.

Some anthropologists, most in fact, have held that the Epulu band was not typical, partly because of the presence of Patrick Putnam. He had come to do his field work there, but had stayed and established a hospital and a kind of hotel for the rare travelers who, in those early days, ventured along that dreadful road linking Stanleyville (as it was still called) to Bunia and the roads south. Later the colonial government established an animal-capturing station at Epulu, and it was alleged that this made the Mbuti of the Epulu territory still further atypical. There is some truth to this argument, and we shall look at it later. But for the moment I shall simply repeat, with the advantage of hindsight, what I said then, namely, that in most essential respects I found little difference between the Epulu Mbuti and any other net-hunting Mbuti *in the forest world*. I think many, though not all, differences

of opinion are due to the changes that have taken place in the years that inter-
vened between the fifties and the seventies. But for the purist, and as a matter of
simple fact, let us take what follows as representative at least, if not only, of the
Epulu band.

THE CONCEPT OF "FAMILY"

Right away I was in trouble. It is almost as though the Mbuti want to confuse
the anthropologist as much as they do the villagers! The band that left the village
and established a temporary camp an hour or so away, on one of my very first visits
into the forest, was in fact only a part of a much larger band that was already en-
camped much deeper in the forest. And, when at the end of a day's march we
arrived in the main camp, I found that some of those who had set out with us and
who had spent the past two weeks in the camp near the village, and before that
had lived in the Mbuti "permanent" camp, had not arrived. They had split off
along the trail somewhere and, I was told, gone to join "in-laws" in other hunting
territories. One of these happened to be across the tribal border and in Bira land,
whereas Epulu itself was an Ndaka village. This, of course, I soon found to be the
normal pattern of fission and fusion, and when the main hunting camp moved, it
in turn divided, some leaving and others joining it from other territories, often
from as many as four or five territories away on either side, and sometimes a good
deal further. The "band" itself then, was never the same in composition from one
month to the next.

Trying to establish the kinship composition of a "band" was a tricky operation.
The Mbuti referred to any one hunting camp as a family, and they applied kinship

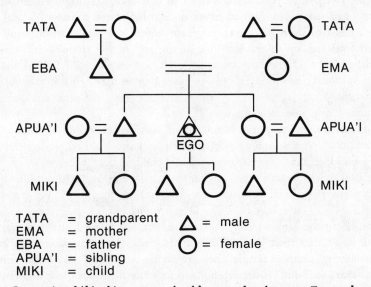

TATA = grandparent
EMA = mother
EBA = father
APUA'I = sibling
MIKI = child

△ = male
○ = female

*Fig. 2: Generational/kinship terms of address and reference. From the point of
view of ego, sexual differentiation is only made at the parental level.*

terms to every single member of that camp. The terminology for address or reference was simple:

Grandparent	*Tata*
Mother/Father	*Ema/Eba*
Sibling	*Apua'i*
Child	*Miki*

One thing to note right away is that gender is only differentiated at the parental level. As far as the Mbuti were concerned, that was the only level where it had any relevance. The sexual relationship prior to marriage, when no children are born, is one thing; between married partners, when children *do* result, it is something totally else. In the first (premarital or, as it proves, extramarital) instance it is of personal and private rather than social and public significance. Only when children are born, or only when children *might* be born, making the sexual act socially significant, did the Mbuti see any need to distinguish gender. Gender, for the Mbuti, was related directly to procreativity. After all, children and elders are incapable of bearing children, and since they are capable of doing all other things equally, without regard to gender, why make the distinction?

As for youths, who, we would say, clearly *are* capable of producing children whether married or not, the Mbuti simply denied the fact and said that although youths could have sex whenever they wanted (within minimal bounds of privacy and respect for others) children would never be born until the youths were married. There was only one restriction that I could discover on the way the sexual act was performed: in premarital or extramarital sex it is forbidden for the partners to embrace each other fully; they must hold each other by the elbows. The distance so induced of course in no way need prevent conception, yet Putnam said that for the twenty-five years he had lived in that area, keeping a record of births and deaths and marriages, he had never once come across a case of a girl giving birth to a child or even becoming pregnant before she was married. And in the years that followed, up to my last visit at the end of the colonial era (and even after independence), I similarly could never document a case of extramarital pregnancy. It may be that some herbal contraceptive is used, though again I could never document the fact, try as I might, and abortion was similarly denied and undocumented as a possible explanation.

The net result however, as the Mbuti saw it, was that every Mbuti child was born within wedlock. That was, they said, because you got married when you *wanted* to have a child. In other words, every Mbuti child is born because he or she was *wanted*. That is the heart of the matter, as the Mbuti see it. Regardless of the technology employed, and the extent to which Putnam and I were deceived or correct, the *belief* is a reality of real and enormous social significance, and immediately makes of the Mbuti family something very special and vitally important. It is a voluntary rather than an involuntary association, so that when they refer to an entire hunting camp as family, they are saying something very important. They are saying that the "band" is something held together by bonds quite different from, almost without regard to, "lineage."

In fact, the only way I could define "family" (or "band"), even going by the usage of kinship terminology, was as "those people who are living together in a single hunting camp and cooperating in the hunt, at any given moment." The moment someone left the camp, even if they were siblings from the same womb, the kinship terms of address and reference were no longer used, but were replaced by personal names. Conversely, when a stranger, totally unrelated by kinship, was accepted into the camp and became a member of that economic unit, he or she was accorded kinship status according to age and marital condition. Even when a band was split up into a number of smaller segments within the same hunting territory, each forming its own small hunting camp (*pa* or *apa*), the same applied, the concept of "family" shrinking accordingly. If we disregard actual kinship, however, we could consider all those hunting within any one recognized territory as a "clan," which may subdivide within the territory into "lineages." I prefer to retain the Mbuti usage and refer to "camps," using the term "band" to refer to all those within any territory, even if divided into several camps.

As the Mbuti saw it the family was primarily of economic significance. The tracing of actual genealogies was made difficult enough by the insistence of the Mbuti that they were "truly" related to every other person in that hunting camp, and had no "real" relatives in other camps, bands, or territories. Whenever they did admit to a relative elsewhere it was usually a sign that they were about to pack up and move to join that relative's camp. Such movement always took place when the monthly general relocation took place, which was when the immediate vicinity had been hunted and gathered to the point that the daily hunt was inconveniently far away from the camp. But even in the middle of the life of any one camp, in the first or second week perhaps, an individual or a family often might suddenly pack up and leave, or another family arrive and settle in. Such movement was of political rather than economic significance. It was a way of averting a major dispute that was brewing between two individuals or families. Mobility was perhaps just as much of political importance as it was economic, and sometimes band movement was determined by the relationship of the band, or of individuals within it, to the village, and to whatever "demands" the village might be making.

KINSHIP AND TERRITORIALITY

There was little property to inherit. As they moved into elderhood adult males relinquished their hunting nets and spears according to the needs of their "sons." Although this generally meant a biological son, it could also be a son-in-law, or one of the classificatory "sons" who happened to be in the camp at that time and in need. A woman tended to hold on to her possessions until she died, but they were equally few and equally easily renewable: a gathering basket and a metal paring knife, and perhaps a machete. At death the tendency was for biological sons to inherit from fathers, daughters from mothers.

At birth a child "inherited" nominal clan membership and its associated totem from her or his father, suggesting a patrilineal system at work. At that time, however, although every Mbuti could recite his or her clan membership and totemic affiliation, and did so readily enough, I was suspicious (and confused). Why, I had to ask myself, were they then so reluctant to make the distinction between "real" and "classificatory" (or fictive) kin? Several times I was scolded for bad manners and "impropriety" for my persistence in pursuing biological relationships to include kin beyond the camp, and even worse, in pursuing them within the camp to demonstrate that some who claimed kinship were not biologically related at all. And then, when cross-checking in other camps, other bands, and other territories, I began coming across the very same individuals that I had met elsewhere, and they not only claimed different kin, but sometimes gave different clan and totemic affiliations. Most often they were those of their mothers, sometimes of their wives, and not all that infrequently, those of a close friend in that camp! Where was the neat, clear-cut kinship system so beloved of anthropology?

Only after my third field trip, each time making Epulu my headquarters but necessarily cross-checking information with territories on either side, was I able to discern some consistency. There was very definitely a tendency for bands to be patrilineal in composition, though this seemed more the case with the archers than with the net-hunters. While in different social contexts any one Mbuti might cite different clan affiliation, I *was* able to trace clan genealogies that made sense. But I could only do this when considering the clan's relationship with the village world, for each clan of village farmers claimed a hereditary relationship with a clan of forest, Mbuti, hunters. Since the villages were very definitely (though not exclusively) patrilineal, patrilocal units, each village saw the adjacent hunting territory as belonging to an equally patrilineal, patrilocal Mbuti clan.

We have already seen that the economic and political realities of forest hunting life demanded a constant population flux and interterritorial movement that completely denied the reality of the village ideal of a localized clan, and as far as I could see that was all that the Mbuti clan system was, a village ideal. For the purposes served by their relationship with the villagers, and no other, the Mbuti traced their descent in the male line and assumed clan names and totems. We shall have to examine this in more detail later, but it is important to establish that in forest context, during those three field trips, I almost *never* heard clan membership or totemic affiliation cited, which is surely a measure of its *effective* insignificance.

We can all trace descent in any way we like; that does not make us patri- or matrilineal. It is only when lineality is manifest in effective ways that we can talk of a "system." There was a tendency for brothers to hunt together; after all, they grew up in the same nuclear family and learned hunting techniques from the same biological father, and on the hunt it is important to know your fellow hunters intimately, if the hunt is to be successful and safe. But it was rare for all brothers (if there were more than two) to be in any one camp or even in any one territory at any one time. Members of any one camp might have, according to my calculations, biological kin, male and female, who were hunting in other territories as far away as one hundred kilometers in either direction. When the "clan" is dispersed over a distance of two hundred kilometers it is difficult for me, in the context of forest hunters, to see it as a very effective sociological unit.

There were no problems of inheritance, since all property was perishable and renewable (hunting nets were constantly being added to, knives and machetes constantly being stolen or "borrowed" from villagers), and on the other crucial

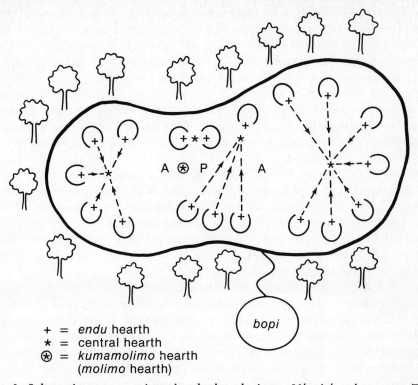

+ = *endu* hearth
* = central hearth
⊛ = *kumamolimo* hearth
(*molimo* hearth)

Fig. 3: Schematic representation of endu *hearths in an Mbuti hunting camp. The Mbuti conception of "family" unites in terms of address all those who hunt together and live in the same camp at any one time. Within such camps, which change in composition as they change location monthly, there are distinct lines of fission and fusion that can be seen by the way the* endu *are clustered, and by their orientation with respect to the central hearths. If the* molimo *is in progress there will be one special central hearth (the* kumamolino*) placed so as to suggest the maximum unity for that camp.*

issue where a kinship system is always invoked, marriage, clan membership was virtually ignored. When a couple were about to get married, the crucial question that was asked was "is your spouse-to-be near or far?" By this both genealogical and territorial distance were meant, for both were important considerations to the Mbuti.

It is consistent with their economic definition of "family" as "those who hunt together in the same camp at any one time" that their primary consideration in marriage should be economic. In marrying "far," in territorial terms, you give yourself the maximum economic and political advantage. In case of dispute you can move to your spouse's territory readily and hunt there, since you will have frequently visited it with your spouse. (Mbuti are loyal to their nuclear families, if not to their lineage or clan!) And the further that territory is from the scene of the dispute, the better. Similarly, if the weather is bad in one part of the forest, spoiling the hunting or gathering, it is highly advantageous to have ready entry into some distant territory well beyond the effects of the local weather system.

Affinal bonds, forged through marriage, are those most exploited to claim the right to hunt in other territories, but almost as frequently exploited are the claims to have a brother or sister, a father or mother, or just a friend, in the camp you wish to join, for whatever reasons. And occasionally people visit just for the sake of visiting, without making any such claims to kinship or friendship, though it would be difficult to find a camp in which you could not make some such claim. Even knowing of someone who is known to someone in the camp you are visiting is considered a valid claim.

So much for a kinship "system," for the moment. I traced many marriages within the nominal clan, though according to the villagers all clans were exogamous. If pressed, the Mbuti simply claimed that actually that clan was divided into subclans that *could* legitimately marry. When considering a proposed marriage the Mbuti never cited clan membership. They merely asked if anyone could remember if the couple's grandparents were related. This effectively prevented the marriage of first cousins on either side.

But if clan, even lineage, were of little consequence, the concept of family was primary. In following any one band throughout the course of the year, I noted that each successive camp, about a dozen in all, was different in size and composition. Significantly, it was also different in shape (see Fig. 4). And it was almost possible to predict the size and shape of the next camp from the size and shape of the first. At first this seems to add to the confusion of the kinship system, but once we abandon the concept of a classical kinship "system" at work, another system immediately comes to light, and one that is much more truly "effective."

When an Mbuti calls another "mother," he or she is acknowledging all the rights and privileges and the duties and obligations proper between a mother and child. The model for social behavior is clearly established in the nuclear family. But quickly, as we have seen, the child learns to address everyone by one or other of the terms he uses within the nuclear family, regardless of kinship but according to *age*. Thus any female Mbuti of the same age level as your mother will be addressed by you as *Ema*, and you will have the same expectations and be able to make the same demands on all those "mothers" that you can on your own. To a certain extent there is even a comparable affective relationship to match the effective bonds. What an incredible system of social security *that* system offers! No matter where you are, in whatever camp in whatever territory, you are bound to a plurality of mothers and fathers and grandparents and siblings and children as powerfully and effectively as if they were your own biological family. There are no such things as orphans, no childless mothers, no solitary children without brothers and sisters, and no lonely old people, for all old people have one immense family to care for them, wherever they are.

THE EDUCATIONAL PROCESS

All of this is learned during infancy, where perhaps the most important lessons of socialization are learned, in the *endu*, the home of the nuclear family. The rela-

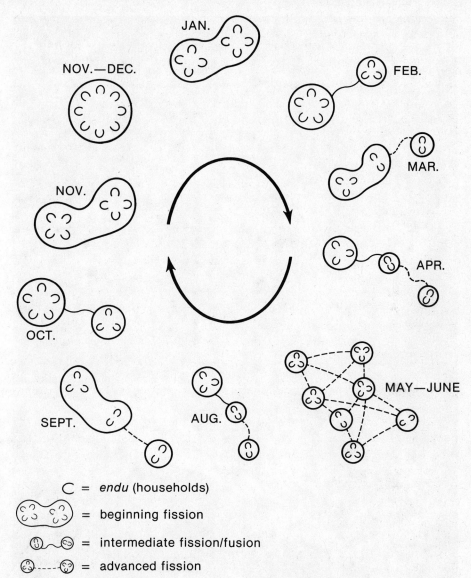

JAN.

NOV.—DEC.

FEB.

MAR.

NOV.

APR.

OCT.

SEPT.

AUG.

MAY—JUNE

C = *endu* (households)

= beginning fission

= intermediate fission/fusion

= advanced fission

Fig. 4: Idealized series of camp changes showing the process of fission and fusion utilized for conflict avoidance during the course of a one-year period.

tionship between affective and effective bonds is the child's first introduction to the realities of the Mbuti economic system, with its emphasis on sharing and cooperation. In the first three years of life every Mbuti alive experiences almost total security. The infant is breast-fed for those three years, and is allowed almost every freedom. Regardless of gender, the infant learns to have absolute trust in both

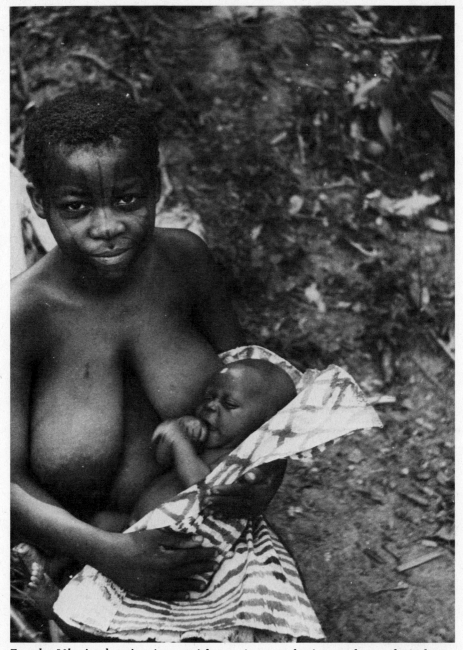

For the Mbuti, education into social consciousness begins at the mother's breast. Here the infant is wrapped in a freshly cut and decorated piece of bark cloth, symbolizing its ultimate dependence on the forest, the mother and father of all.

male and female parent. If anything, the father is just another kind of mother, for in the second year the father formally introduces the child to its first solid food. There used to be a beautiful ritual in which the mother presented the child to the father in the middle of the camp, where all important statements are made (anyone speaking from the middle of the camp must be listened to). The father took the child and held it to his breast, and the child would try to suckle, crying *"ema, ema,"* or "mother." The father would shake his head, and say "no, father . . . *eba,"* but like a mother (the Mbuti said), then give the child its first solid food.

At three the child ventures out into the world on its own and enters the *bopi,* what we might call a playground, a tiny camp perhaps a hundred yards from the main camp, often on the edge of a stream. The *bopi* were indeed playgrounds, and often very noisy ones, full of fun and high spirits. But they were also rigorous training grounds for eventual economic responsibility. On entry to the *bopi,* for one thing, the child discovers the importance of age as a structural principle, and the relative unimportance of gender and biological kinship. The *bopi* is the private world of the children. Younger youths may occasionally venture in, but if adults or elders try, as they sometimes do when angry at having their afternoon snooze interrupted, they invariably get driven out, taunted, and ridiculed. Children, among the Mbuti, have rights, but they also learn that they have responsibilities. Before the hunt sets out each day it is the children, sometimes the younger youths, who light the hunting fire.

Ritual among the Mbuti is often so informal and apparently casual that it may pass unnoticed at first. Yet insofar as ritual involves symbolic acts that represent unspoken, perhaps even unthought, concepts or ideals, or invoke other states of being, alternative frames of mind and reference, then Mbuti life is full of ritual. The hunting fire is one of the more obvious of such rituals. Early in the morning children would take firebrands from the *bopi,* where they always lit their own fire with embers from their family hearths, and set off on the trail by which the hunt was to leave that day (the direction of each day's hunt was always settled by discussion the night before). Just a short distance from the camp they lit a fire at the base of a large tree, and covered it with special leaves that made it give off a column of dense smoke. Hunters leaving the camp, both men and women, and such youths and children as were going with them, had to pass by this fire. Some did so casually, without stopping or looking, but passing through the smoke. Others reached into the smoke with their hands as they passed, rubbing the smoke into their bodies. A few always stopped, for a moment, and let the smoke envelop them, only then almost dreamily moving off.

And indeed it *was* a form of intoxication, for the smoke invoked the spirit of the forest, and by passing through it the hunters sought to fill themselves with that spirit, not so much to make the hunt successful as to minimize the sacrilege of killing. Yet they, the hunters, could not light the fire themselves. After all, they were already contaminated by death. Even youths, who daily joined the hunt at the edges, catching any game that escaped the nets, by hand, if they could, were not pure enough to invoke the spirit of forestness. But young children were uncontaminated, as yet untainted by contact with the original sin of the Mbuti. It was their

When children tire of playing in the bopi they are always welcome with their many mothers and fathers in the main camp.

Before the day's hunt all hunters pass through the hunting fire, lit by children.
Sometimes they sit down beside the fire, as if washing themselves in the sacred
smoke.

responsibility to light the fire, and if it was not lit then the hunt would not take
place, or as the Mbuti put it, the hunt *could* not take place.

In this way even the children in Mbuti society, at the first of the four age levels
that dominate Mbuti social structure, are given very real social responsibility and
see themselves as a part of that structure, by virtue of their purity. After all, they
have just been born from the source of all purity, the forest itself. By the same
reasoning, the elders, who are about to return to that ultimate source of all being,
through death, are at least closer to purity than the adults, who are daily contaminated by killing. Elders no longer go on the hunt. So, like the children, the elders
have important sacred ritual responsibilities in the Mbuti division of labor by age.

In the *bopi* the children play, but they have no "games" in the strict sense of the word. Levi-Strauss has perceptively compared games with rituals, suggesting that whereas in a game the players start theoretically equal but end up unequal, in a ritual just the reverse takes place. All are equalized. Mbuti children could be seen every day playing in the *bopi*, but not once did I see a game, not one activity that smacked of any kind of competition, except perhaps that competition that it is necessary for us all to feel from time to time, competition with our own private and personal inadequacies. One such pastime (rather than game) was tree climbing. A dozen or so children would climb up a young sapling. Reaching the top, their weight brought the sapling bending down until it almost touched the ground. Then all the children leapt off together, shrieking as the young tree sprang upright again with a rush. Sometimes one child, male or female, might stay on a little too long, either out of fear, or out of bravado, or from sheer carelessness or bad timing. Whatever the reason, it was a lesson most children only needed to be taught once, for the result was that you got flung upward with the tree, and were lucky to escape with no more than a few bruises and a very bad fright.

Other pastimes taught the children the rules of hunting and gathering. Frequently elders, who stayed in camp when the hunt went off, called the children into the main camp and enacted a mock hunt with them there. Stretching a discarded piece of net across the camp, they pretended to be animals, showing the children how to drive them into the nets. And, of course, the children played house, learning the patterns of cooperation that would be necessary for them later in life. They also learned the prime lesson of egality, other than for purposes of division of labor making no distinction between male and female, this nuclear family or that. All in the *bopi* were *apua'i* to each other, and so they would remain throughout their lives. At every age level—childhood, youth, adulthood, or old age—everyone of that level is *apua'i* to all the others. Only adults sometimes (but so rarely that I think it was only done as a kind of joke, or possibly insult) made the distinction that the Bira do, using *apua'i* for male and *amua'i* for female. Male or female, for the Mbuti, if you are the same age you are *apua'i*, and that means that you share everything equally, regardless of kinship or gender.

YOUTH AND POLITICS

Sometime before the age of puberty boys or girls, whenever they feel ready, move back into the main camp from the *bopi* and join the youths. This is when they must assume new responsibilities, which for the youths are primarily political. Already, in the *bopi*, the children become involved in disputes, and are sometimes instrumental in settling them by ridicule, for nothing hurts an adult more than being ridiculed publicly by children. The art of reason, however, is something they learn from the youths, and it is the youths who apply the art of reason to the settlement of disputes.

When puberty comes it separates them, for the first time in their experience, from each other as *apua'i*. Very plainly girls are different from boys. When a girl has her first menstrual period the whole camp celebrates with the wild *elima*

Youths are responsible for settling disputes and are constantly critical of adult behavior. Here they criticize the way adult males kept the best honey for themselves.

festival, in which the girl, and some of her chosen girl friends, are the center of all attention, living together in a special *elima* house. Male youths sit outside the *elima* house and wait for the girls to come out, usually in the afternoon, for the *elima* singing. They sing in antiphony, the girls leading, the boys responding. Boys come from neighboring territories all around, for this is a time of courtship. But there are always eligible youths within the camp as well, and the *elima* girl may well choose girls from other territories to come and join her, so there is more than enough excuse for every youth to carry on several flirtations, legitimate or illegitimate. I have known even first cousins to flirt with each other, but learned to be prudent enough not to pull out my kinship charts and point this out—well, not in public anyway.

The *elima* is more than a premarital festival, more than a joint initiation of youth into adulthood, and more than a rite of passage through puberty, though it is all those things. It is a public recognition of the opposition of male and female, and every *elima* is used to highlight the *potential* for conflict that lies in that opposition. As at other times of crisis, at puberty, a time of change and uncertainty, the Mbuti bring all the major forms of conflict out into the open. And the one that evidently most concerns them is the male/female opposition.

The adults begin to play a special form of "tug of war" that is clearly a ritual rather than a game. All the men are on one side, the women on the other. At first it

Akidinimba during her final elima *dance, after which public opinion coerced her into marriage. Dances of the* elima *girls make public the responsibility of adult womanhood, while the choreography, like the musical form, emphasizes special patterns of cooperation.*

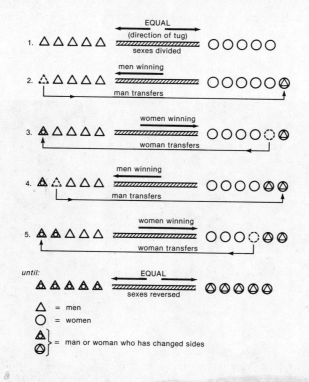

Fig. 5: Tug of war. This is one of the Mbuti's many techniques of conflict resolution, involving role reversal and the principle of opposition without hostility.

looks like a game, but quickly it becomes clear that the objective is for *neither* side to win. As soon as the women begin to win, one of them will leave the end of the line and run around to join the men, assuming a deep male voice and in other ways ridiculing manhood. Then, as the men begin to win, a male will similarly join the women, making fun of womanhood as he does so. Each adult on changing sides attempts to outdo all the others in ridiculing the opposite sex. Finally, when nearly all have switched sides, and sexes, the ritual battle between the genders simply collapses into hysterical laughter, the contestants letting go of the rope, falling onto the ground, and rolling over with mirth. Neither side wins, both are equalized very nicely, and each learns the essential lesson, that there should be *no* contest.

ADULTHOOD AND ECONOMY

It is significant that this is primarily an adult activity, though the youths may mock it and even imitate it as a way of ridiculing the adults. That is because adults are generally considered to be the most troublesome members of any camp. This is inevitable, but making it plain and overt helps to offset what might, in other circumstances, quickly become a tendency toward the domination of Mbuti society

As they get close to the place where the hunting nets will be set up, men and male youths tend to come together in small groups. Except in rare patches of sunlight, as here, the Mbuti are barely visible against the forest background.

by the adults, who are, after all, the hunters and gatherers, the food providers, and the life givers. But then, the youths will argue (joined by the elders—the alternate generation principle at work), it is the adults who are the cause of all the "noise," all that goes wrong in the camp. For they are the killers of animals, and killing is the greatest "noise" of all. It is as though the adults sense this ambivalence themselves, for every day they bring back the food that all Mbuti clamor for and enjoy with such relish, yet it is they who daily renew the hard fact of man's mortality. And although women do not kill, they do participate in the hunt. Children and elders *can* go on the hunt, but they are never an integral part of it, and have no position or role other than as bystanders.

Apart from being the major economic activity, the most dramatic event of everyday life, the hunt is also the greatest sacrilege in the life of the Mbuti, and full of inherent conflict. To some extent this is ritualized and turned to advantage.

Among the net hunters, after passing through the hunting fire the men and women moved on, perhaps only a short distance, or perhaps an hour or more away from the camp, depending on how long they had been hunting in that area. They used to straggle out of the camp in no apparent order, each heading in his or her own way to the place where the first hunt of the day was to start. Women gathered as they went, and even when in place, waiting for the men to set up the nets, they continued to look around for nuts, mushrooms, and berries, or the sweet *itaba* roots that are such a delicacy. What they gathered in this way actually formed the bulk of the daily diet, and certainly added to the variety of ways in which the game could be cooked and served, but little glamour attached to gathering, and the women, just as much as the men, found the hunt exciting. Despite its dangers there were seldom even minor injuries, and most of those came about through carelessness.

While the women were filling their baskets with vegetable produce the men set up their nets, over three feet high and up to a hundred yards long, in a huge semicircle. It was impossible to see the length of any one net, yet all the men positioned themselves and started setting their nets up at the same time, each unfolding his net and hanging it on low shrubs or saplings until he came to where his neighbor had started hanging his net. The precision was as remarkable as that of the women, who by then had also taken up position, silently. At a given signal they began beating in towards the nets, whooping and yelling, striking the ground with bundles of leaves and sticks. The game put up in this way mostly fled towards the nets, rarely would it double back through the line of advancing women, though sometimes big game—a leopard or a buffalo—might do that. If big game was sighted the women cried out a warning to the men, who lowered the nets to let the game through, rather than risk having it tear its way through, destroying a good net.

The nets snared everything from the smallest duikers to the largest antelopes. Some game, usually the heavy game, often tried to escape to the side, where the semicircle of nets ended. That was where the youths positioned themselves, with spears or bows and arrows, or as often as not, simply with their bare hands. This was the chance for a male youth to prove himself as a hunter and, by presenting a large antelope caught with his own hands to the parents of his girl friend, win their approval for him to marry her. But whereas the adults were all shouting and making a lot of noise to scare and confuse the game, the youths remained silent, hidden, until their turn came.

I mention this because the Mbuti used the word *akami*, meaning "noise," to mean not only noise, but also conflict; fighting within a tightly cooperative camp can spoil a hunt just as effectively as too much noise at the wrong moment. Silence, or *ekimi*, is the preferred quality of "peace." The adults, caught in the dilemma of having to kill to survive, were also caught in the dilemma of having to create *akami* in order to succeed as hunters. And adulthood, as I have said, is regarded as a time of *akami*, of noise and conflict. Even though involved at the edges of the hunt, the youths managed to remain aloof, and to retain the positive value of *ekimi*.

TECHNIQUES OF CONFLICT RESOLUTION

This was as it should be, for the role of youth in the Mbuti division of labor is the role of politician. They are the lawmakers and the judges. That is also as it should be, for there is little cause for conflict in the life of youth. More important still, the best singers and dancers are to be found among the youth, and dance and song are the prime means by which Mbuti regulate the good and the bad in their lives. Just as children are by their very nature best fitted for the sacred role, lighting the hunting fire, because they have just come from the source of all sanctity, and just as the adults are best equipped for the economic role in life, being at the height of their physical capabilities, so are the youth deemed best fitted for the political role. They have not yet become hunters, bringing death to all living creatures. They are not yet well-enough developed for that role; they will become hunters when they marry. But they have the vigor and vision of youth. They are the singers and dancers. And above all, the future is theirs.

Recognizing change as inherent in their way of life, the Mbuti avoid codifying behavior into what is right and what is wrong. At any one time there is a general consensus as to right behavior, which is what is right for that moment. But if a question or dispute arises then judgment is given only in terms of what is right for the band, or camp, as a whole. Ultimately that means what is right for the forest, the ultimate arbiter. Right and wrong are not inherent in any action; right and wrong can only be determined by the effect of any action.

This does not mean that the rules of behavior are vague, or are so fluid as to have little meaning. Often the rules are very specific, and as long as they work for the general good they remain unchanged. But as the context changes, as it did when the villagers first moved into the forest, and still more dramatically under colonial rule, the rules change. I saw them changing as the Belgians increasingly encouraged commercial exploitation of the forest, changing the relationship between hunter and villager, even between hunter and forest. And as independence approached there were heady decisions to be made: whether to spend more or less time in the village, where contact could be had with the modern world that was closing in around them. And always it was the youths who made the decisions, for, as the elders said, the future was theirs to live in.

Even when it came to settling disputes this fell largely to the youths, for through their music they were associated with the positive value of *ekimi*. However loud a forest song may be, it is never "noisy" in the Mbuti sense.

Mbuti music is highly integrative. The very musical structure and form and the techniques of singing reproduce, almost exactly, the patterns of cooperation required in whatever aspect of real life that particular kind of song relates to. Thus *elima* songs are sung in antiphony, with the girls taking the lead, representing the coming division of the sexes, but also the fact that it is an opposition devoid of hostility. Among themselves the *elima* girls sing in parallel seconds, illustrating the ideal kinds of relationships they should have with each other, the closest kind of friendship and intimacy (something that the males do not need, it seems). The hunting songs are always sung in round form, and in canon, and utilize the hoquet technique, by which the melodic line is broken up into separate notes, each sung by one hunter, so that the melody cannot be made to sound unless all the hunters sing their individual notes, with precision and at exactly the right moment. The hunting song thus recreates the intensive cooperative patterns required by the hunt, and like the hunt the grouping is circular, with women forming one semicircle around the fire, men forming an opposing semicircle, with youths on each side where the two semicircles almost join.

So it is with the other two major modes of Mbuti music; each reinforces the appropriate patterns for the corresponding activity. One is a gathering song (particularly for the honey season) and the other a death song. All four forms of song demand cooperation; not one of them can be produced by a single singer. The only solo song that is possible is the lullaby, an intimate communication between a mother and her child, to be sung by her alone and composed specially for each child while it is yet in the womb.

THE *MOLIMO* AND "JUSTICE"

While the youths do not sing a prominent part in the hunting song, any more than their active role in the hunt is prominent, they dominate the other song forms. Of these the *molimo* songs are the most powerful, for the *molimo* represents the spirit of the forest itself, and in all times of major crisis it is invoked by song. For this song to be heard by the forest it must be sung by an unmarried youth, into a trumpet that transforms the sound into something quite unearthly.

As the adults sing around the fire at night, trying to restore *ekimi*, the youths slip out of the camp and go to where the *molimo* trumpet is hidden, high up in a tree. They take it down, bathe it in a stream where it will be kept, night after night, until the crisis is ended, when it will be restored to its hiding place in the *molimo* tree. The youths then wrap it in leaves so that it looks like a part of the forest. It may be anything from six to fifteen feet long, but as they come into camp *all* the youths will have one hand on it, symbolizing their unanimity. One of their number,

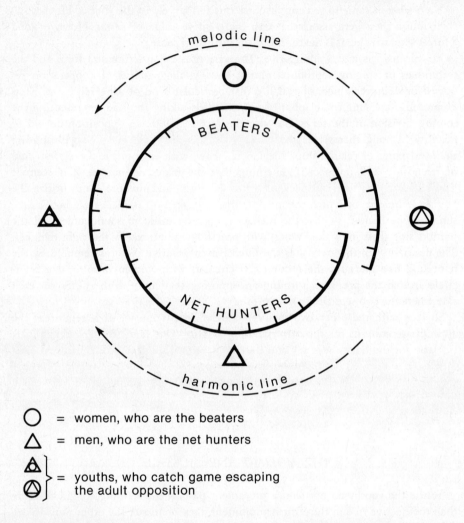

Fig. 6: Hunting song. The musical form and singing technique used for the hunting songs clearly reproduce the intensive patterns of cooperation demanded by the hunt itself. The singing takes place around a central hearth, just as the hunters, during the hunt, surround their quarry.

the one considered by all to have the most beautiful voice, sings into one end of the trumpet. Sometimes he will make leopard sounds, and sometimes break into the shrill trumpeting of an elephant. These represent, respectively, the forces of life and death. The youths and the trumpet sit by the fire with the adults and elders, singing with them, or move about the camp, as they wish.

The adults and even the elders are powerless to sing the crisis away, however well they sing. They are too impure, too filled with *akami*. But if they try hard enough and sing well enough, the molimo *will* come into the camp. Many is the night that I have been off with the youths, waiting for the adults to get themselves together, and never have the youths brought the *molimo* into the camp if they did not feel the men were working hard enough and singing well enough.

The occasion for a *molimo mangbo*, a great *molimo*, is usually death, and the objective is for the elders, adults, and youths to sing every night, for at least a month, all through the hours of darkness, making sure that the forest "is awake," as they put it, and aware of their plight. If they can be sure that the forest is awake, and not asleep, then they know that the dead person will be safe, and the only way they can be sure is to invoke the *molimo* itself into their midst. If there has been any fighting among the adults, poor hunting, illicit flirtation, or adultery, then the youths simply leave them singing in the camp and carry the *molimo* around the fringes of the camp, making it sound for all the world like a herd of elephant just waiting to come in and destroy the camp, as indeed elephant can do with ease. But if the adults sing well, and that means if they cooperate with each other in the difficult technique of the *molimo* songs, then the youth who is singing into the trumpet will take the song of the adults and softly echo it, the trumpet transforming the sound into something totally different, nonhuman, endowed with power, the power and vitality of youth, and pass it on to the forest.

Of course everyone knows who is doing the singing, and in real life he might be an absolute rascal. Even when the youths bring the *molimo* into the camp they often clown around. But symbols thrive under such conditions, and when the youths finally take the *molimo* out of the camp before dawn, and it can be heard getting further and further away, it is as though they have taken the profane song of mere adults and transformed it into something infinitely sacred, something so utterly beautiful and full of the *ekimi* of youth that the forest itself must awaken and rejoice, and bring *ekimi* to all its *miki*, or children, including the one who has died.

If the occasion is of lesser importance, such as a simple dispute in the ordinary course of everyday camp life, then there is what is called a *molimo madé*, or a "lesser" *molimo*. For this the adults do not sing; more than likely they are the culprits. But the youths who are displeased with something that has happened take matters into their own hands. They may have tried open criticism first, and ridicule. They may even have persuaded the children to come in and ridicule an adult culprit. But if none of this works, then one night, when everyone else is sleeping, the youths slip silently out of the camp, get the *molimo* trumpet, and creep back to the edge of the camp. Then the first thing the sleeping Mbuti know, men and women, elders and children alike, is that there is an angry elephant somewhere close by, first on this side of the camp, then that. Sometimes it sounds like more than one.

After the first few elephant cries on the *molimo* everyone knows that it is not a real elephant, but that does not mean it is any less dangerous. If any are sleeping outside they run inside and pull the leaf doors tight shut. There may be shouts of protest, telling the *molimo* to go away. Sometimes adults will actually name

Youth and music to resolve conflict among adults.

youths and swear at them for waking them up, but that is to invite certain disaster. The youths move in, again with the *molimo* trumpet decorated like "the spirit of the forest," or "the animal of the forest." But unlike when they come in with the *molimo mangbo*, so unobtrusively that often I have not known it until the trumpet was at the fire right beside me, the *molimo madé* moves in with a rush and a harsh trumpeting. It charges about the camp, every youth holding onto it as though it were pulling them this way and that rather than the other way around. The angry animal of the forest destroys anything in its path. It tramples out fires. It destroys any little stick seats or beds that might have been left outside. Meat-drying racks may be torn from the ground, and every house in the camp is subjected to a battering. Some even have leaves torn off the roof, sticks pulled out of the ground, the house frame damaged, and, I am told (I never saw it happen), sometimes totally destroyed.

Under such provocation the bolder adults, male or female, run out into the camp and shout and swear at the youths, but then the forest animal may simply turn and charge them, knocking them over or driving them back into their houses. The adults are impotent; even the elders, normally highly respected, and whose role is usually that of arbitrator, counselor, adviser, can do nothing to stop this wild rampage of youth when it is reacting to *akami* in the camp.

Here we see a typically diffuse sense of law and justice, common to so many hunting societies, at work. Perhaps the adult hunters had decided to end the band's stay down in the village earlier than suited the youths. This was the kind of thing that was beginning to happen just before independence. The youths wanted to know what was going on. They were interested in the schools that they were told were going to be opened to Mbuti children. They wanted a good look at foreigners who came along the road. Some even traveled to the administrative posts to see for themselves how "civilized" people lived, so they could judge whether that was what they wanted for themselves or not. They needed to stay longer in the village world at that time. But the adults were impatient. Their job was to hunt, and after a few days in a village they wanted to go back into the forest, and whether the youths liked it or not sometimes they did just that, leaving the youths behind. In those days the youths never brought a *molimo mangbo* into their village camps, and only very rarely did I ever see or hear a *molimo madé* there. The youths would wait until they returned to the forest; *then* they would let the adults know who were the lawgivers, who decided what was right and was was wrong!

But if any one individual adult had been responsible, or if the *molimo madé* had been brought out just because one married couple was creating a lot of *akami* in the camp by constantly squabbling, the *molimo* never singled out such individual wrongdoers for attack, to the exclusion of others. Just as every youth had to have a hand on the trumpet, signifying that the youths were united and unanimous, so the animal of the forest attacked every house in the camp, as if to say that everyone shared in the blame for having allowed the *akami* to grow in their midst. The blame, in this way, was always distributed among all members of the hunting family, the ideal of the cooperative, egalitarian economic family preserved, and *ekimi* restored.

ELDERS AND ARBITRATION

It was at moments like this that the elders came into prominence. In the Mbuti scheme of things age was clearly the dominant principle of social organization, with territory hard on its heels, then gender, and kinship lagging behind. The responsibility allocated to childhood was that of ritual purification, most specifically in the daily act of lighting the hunting fire. The youths had full control of the political arena, and the adults were fully occupied with all the major economic responsibilities. The role of the elders was the one, as vital as all the others, of socialization. During the daytime, when youths and adults were off on the hunt, the elders mostly stayed behind in the camp, looking after the young children. By playing with them, acting out great sagas of the hunting and gathering days of yore, or just by lying back under the trees and telling stories, old women and men, the *tata* of the camp, filled the youngsters with their own love of the forest, their trust in it, and their respect for the forest values that made life so good.

But when a dispute flared up and the *molimo madé* came into the camp on a nocturnal rampage, while the adults would shout accusations and excuses, it was always the quiet voice of the elders that put the dispute into perspective and showed *why* things had gone wrong. The criticism the youths voiced in physical action the elders reinforced in words, appealing to the supreme value of *ekimi* and citing precedent after precedent. Having lived as long as they had, they could recall one incident after another to support their argument. In extreme cases they would walk to the middle of the camp and criticize individuals by name. But as though such pinpointing of fault were in itself a fault, the elders themselves frequently softened their criticism with sly humor or even open ridicule. The *molimo madé*, then, was a major and recurrent occasion on which the elders could reinforce the Mbuti norms and values, revitalizing the very basis of sociality not just for the children, but for the youths and adults as well.

GENDER, SEX, AND MARRIAGE

While considering conflict let us go back for a moment to the *elima*, for it is towards the end of youth that the Mbuti have their first real personal taste of conflict. In childhood and early youth the only form of conflict they have known has been during the socialization process, as they have learned the hard but necessary lesson that the individual good not only must always be subordinated to the social good, but that ultimately the individual good *is* the social good, and that what is good for the forest is good for all. Since this is a reality rather than an empty platitude for the Mbuti, once the discipline is learned it is easy to bear, though their powerful individualities continue to get in the way every now and then, causing *akami*. That this mainly happens in adulthood is not surprising, and much of the *akami* of adulthood is related to that basic opposition discovered at puberty, the opposition of male and female.

At puberty the youths discover that the ideal of being *apua'i* equally to all others of the same age simply is not possible any longer. Now a boy and a girl can love each other in a way that in simplest terms of physiology is not possible between boy and boy or girl and girl. There was, I noticed, a very definite, if strange sense of infidelity when a youth had an affair with an *apua'i* of the opposite sex. It smacked of preferential treatment. The ideal of equality so carefully nurtured in childhood was suddenly brought into question, and the infidelity that was felt was felt with respect to that ideal.

To some extent this was offset, for the boys at least, by the fact that they tended to sleep together at night, clustered in heaps of warm, nearly naked bodies around a fire in the middle of the camp, or else in an improvised "bachelor hut." As among the girls, there was a great deal of holding and hugging, even in broad daylight. Yet not once, even at night, was I able to detect any evidence of homosexual intercourse either among boys or girls, despite this overt and conscious physical display of affection. But more and more male youths found themselves together, with the male hunters, say, while the female youths were off with the women, gathering. The division of labor functioned, in a way, to relieve something of the infidelity implicit in heterosexual intimacy, but the conflict was clearly there.

Then, when a boy and a girl, perhaps a couple who had come to know each other sexually during the *elima*, decided that they wanted to have children, the conflict was heightened. During an *elima* the *bamelima* ("girls of the *elima* house") invite the male youths of their choice to sleep with them in the *elima* house. They do this by whipping them with young saplings, which they hold demurely by their sides as they sit in the camp and sing with the boys, until they suddenly make a concerted attack on the expectant youths. Then, that evening, the boys who have been whipped must fight their way into the *elima* house, and it is the mothers they have to fight with. Most Mbuti mothers are a great deal stronger and tougher than their sons, so if any mother does not want her son to sleep with a girl, or the other way around, she can make things rough for the boys.

One youth never made it; he was always caught by the women, thrashed and beaten and even taken and thrown into the river. They had good reason: he smoked marijuana to excess, and was hopeless on a hunt. Endeku is now over fifty years old and is still a bachelor.

Endeku in this way escaped the ultimate infidelity of marriage. It is bad enough to show your sexual preference for one over another of your *apua'i*, but to marry and have children removes you still further from all those others with whom you were equally closely bound. On marriage, which for the Mbuti means that a young couple (generally with their parents' approval) simply build a house of their own and start living together, the two youths immediately move from the age level of youth into that of adulthood, from *ekimi* to *akami*. This is not to say that marriage is regarded as undesirable—far from it. With a very few exceptions, like Endeku, every Mbuti wants to marry, to live a long life with one spouse, and to have lots of children. Marriages endure through all the normal trials and troubles, and the affection between spouses seems as tender in old age as when they were blushing newlyweds. But their new responsibilities as adults, their economic rather than political role, is yet another thing that removes them from the *apua'i* they leave behind. Ultimately they will all be together again, but for a brief moment the link is weakened, if not broken.

Once again the Mbuti find a typically unusual way of helping to alleviate, if not avert the conflict. They say that no mother can become pregnant for three years after giving birth to a child, because she must breast-feed it for that time. So they have a rule, one of their very few rules, that after a woman has given birth to a child she may not have sexual relations with her husband for three years. It does not say that she cannot have them with anyone else, and it places no restriction on the husband's extramarital activities. But as we have seen, however they manage it (and I can only repeat again that they *do*) children are never born as a result of extramarital liaisons. So whereas the mother was fully occupied with her new-born child, and as far as I could see, and according to what both the men and women said, hardly ever "slept around," the young husband was not so confined. He generally went back to spending much of his spare time with his old *apua'i* who were still youths, and sleeping as a youth with some of his former girl friends.

So long as he was discreet about this nobody minded, but such friendships often gave rise to much *akami*. For one thing, the married man was unfair competition for male youths who had yet to find wives for themselves, and for another, his wife, if a normal Mbuti, would soon become intensely jealous if her husband proved too popular with her formal rivals. Disputes of this kind were most common among adults, particularly the younger ones who still had *apua'i* among the youths.

It is no wonder then that in their religious life the Mbuti ritualized this potential and experienced conflict in so many ways. I have already described the tug of war, a ritual battle between the sexes. Even more dramatic was *ekokomea*, a dance that always occurred during a *molimo mangbo* as part of the almost anarchic reversal that so frequently accompanies any rite of passage. For the Mbuti it was as though death were itself a reversal, an abnormality which could only be put right by reversing everything else. *Ekokomea* was such a reversal technique, and, like the tug of war, it made gender the focal point. Men drew their bark cloths up tight between their legs, in the manner of women, and women dropped theirs low in the manner of men. Each then, to the accompaniment of the *ekokomea* music, began to ridicule the others as they danced. Women ridiculed manhood by putting enormous lumps of wood into their bark cloths, and they swung these back and forth as they danced around, like enormous ungainly testicles between their legs. This was really hitting where it hurt, and the men were not to be outdone. Their favorite way of ridiculing womanhood was to pretend that they had pots of water and were continually washing *very* smelly private parts. As with the tug of war, each individual sought to outdo the others in his or her mime and ridicule, and before long the whole camp would have joined in and the dancers would end in convulsions on the ground, laughing as much at themselves as at anyone else. By expressing the latent conflict, it was to a large extent expelled, and the norm of sexual differentiation was reinforced.

This is perhaps the most basic of all areas of latent conflict in any society. Like age, another major area of potential conflict, it is biologically determined. The Mbuti find that ritual, public, and frequent manifestation of the conflict is the best way to avert it. It runs throughout the *molimo mangbo* festival, the greatest of all the Mbuti religious occasions. At first, perhaps for a whole month, it may seem that this is exclusively the province of men. All women and children must retire into their houses and close the doors after the evening meal has been eaten, and they must stay there until daybreak. The males sing the songs; the males eat the special food collected from each household for the nightly feasting around the *kumamolimo* (literally, "the vagina of the molimo") hearth in the center of the camp. It is the male youths who handle and control the trumpet. It is as if only the males had the power to sing the forest awake, to sing the dead person to a safe passage in the other world.

But before the *molimo* ends, after a month or so of this show of apparent male dominance, one night an old woman, usually a stranger from another territory, comes into the camp. She is joined by *elima* girls (both beyond the possibility of giving birth to children) at the *kumamolimo*. There they proceed to take over the song. The old woman ties up the men with the twine from which hunting nets are made. As she loops the twine around the necks of the singers, they stop singing, and as they stop the young girls take over. The girls also seize the *banja*, sacred wooden sticks the Mbuti brush together during the molimo. The males are impotent. Their "fire of life" is now in the hands of the women.

Then the old woman circles the fire, and slowly begins to dance deliberately right through it, trampling it and scattering the embers and burning logs as she goes. The men leap into action, kick all the logs and coals back into place, and perform an erotic dance around the fire, as if regenerating life itself. The fire catches hold and blazes upwards, and the old woman merely repeats her dance of destruction. The female takeover only ends when the men make some sign of submission and pay a symbolic fee to regain their control of the *molimo*. Then the nooses are removed from their necks, and the *banja* and the song restored to them together with their male power. But it has been made clear that the power really lies in the hand of Woman, who not only has the power that no man has, to give birth to life, but who also has the power to trample out the fire of life, to bring death.

There are legends of how the women first owned the fire, or first owned the *molimo*, and of how the men had to steal these from them, but these legends are seldom told. There is no need. All that, and a great deal more, is said every time there is a *molimo*.

And now it becomes even more significant that, during those colonial days, the *molimo mangbo* was never held when the Mbuti were staying in their "permanent" camp at the edge of the village. This was the clearest expression of all that for them the forest world was sacred, and the world of the village profane. Even when in the depths of the forest, if a *molimo* festival was held, the trail leading off to the direction of the village world would be closed—just by a symbolic twig perhaps, nothing that would stop a tortoise. But was a sign that for them, at this most sacred of all moments, the profane world simply did not exist and was of no consequence.

It is time now to look at that profane world, for it *does* exist. And in their own inimitable way the Mbuti have adapted to its presence—by keeping the two worlds separate, by being one thing in one world, and something else in the other.

3/The village world

OUTPOSTS OF "CIVILIZATION"

Even at the height of colonial domination the sedentary village world of the Mbutis' neighbors, the immigrant farmers, was able to retain much of its traditional way of life and thought. The road that was built in the thirties from Kisangani (then Stanleyville) to Bunia, branching south to Beni and the Kivu region, was at its best hazardous, and more frequently was impassable at several points simultaneously along its length. Commercial truckers and government workers alike were frequently stranded for days or even weeks. From the point of view of the villagers communications were no better than when all travel was done on foot. Each village retained its sense of isolation even from its closest neighbors. Each village was also largely autonomous, despite the attempt of the colonial power to impose central control through a series of government-appointed chiefs. Tribal unity was still largely nominal, for on being forced into the forest the tribes had split and subdivided, each segment seeking its own way to survive in what for them was such a hostile environment.

The government-appointed chiefs were accorded little respect, and were used by the villagers as a convenient buffer to keep the unwelcome colonials at a distance. In much the same way that the Mbuti sought to keep the villagers out of the central forest, scattered around the periphery, so the villagers accepted the appointed chiefs and used them to keep the government agents confined to their administrative posts, often hundreds of kilometers apart. It was only around these posts that the hand of colonialism was readily evident. It was there that the few colonials seeking to make money through coffee growing had their plantations. It was there that you would find the major mission posts, though a very few missions did establish themselves away from government centers, forming their own little enclaves of colonialism. The government was only too glad to leave it to the appointed chiefs to carry out their will, just as the missions tended to rely on converts trained as catechists to spread their various gospels.

The main aim of the government as far as the villagers were concerned was to maintain the uneasy peace that had fallen on the forest, following on the fighting and mutual suspicion left in the wake of Stanley and the slave traders. Physical violence was the major crime in colonial eyes, and all incidents of such violence were to be dealt with through the government chiefs and tribunals. Serious cases of violence and all cases of murder were to be dealt with only at the administrative posts. Other than keeping the peace, then, the government-appointed chiefs' main responsibility was to collect taxes. These could be paid in cash or kind, and closely linked to taxation was the pressure brought on villagers to grow cotton.

THE DEMANDS OF VILLAGE ECONOMY

This was perhaps one of the major changes introduced by colonialism, and it altered village life in several ways. For one thing, the forest soil is fragile, and cotton exhausted it more rapidly than any of the traditional crops. This meant that plantations had to shift more frequently than before, ultimately growing so far from the village that the village itself had to be relocated. Fresh plantations were cut about every three years, and villages moved every ten years or so. This was a lateral shifting from side to side, always within the peripheral boundaries of the corresponding Mbuti hunting territory, so that each village retained constant ties, such as they were, with the amorphous hunting band within that territory.

It was in another way that taxation and cotton introduced a major change into the relationship between the Mbuti and the villagers. Growing enough food for their own needs was a full-time occupation. Each villager had his own plantations of rice, plantains, and manioc, as well as plots where other vegetable foods were grown. These required constant attention. The government demand for cotton, as a cash crop, could only be met with more labor, and the Mbuti were the only source of labor available. Cotton changed the whole nature of the relationship between the two peoples. Until then it had been one of mutual convenience, for the villagers *could* have gone into the forest themselves to hunt and gather and collect the materials necessary for housing and clothing, but for the most part they preferred to let the Mbuti bring them what they needed. From the Mbuti point of view this was an easy and cheap way of keeping their forest world to themselves. But now the villagers had a very real need for Mbuti labor, without which they could not survive under the colonial regime. And now the relationship became more genuinely burdensome to the Mbuti, for they not only did not like to stay away from their forest for more than few days at a time, they were subject to sickness and heat prostration if they remained in the village world for too long, and work in the open plantations posed a serious threat to their health.

Their resentment was heightened by yet another unintended by-product of the colonial policy. Since the colonial government recognized the virtual impossibility of effectively taxing the nomadic Mbuti, they were not taxed. Some Mbuti perceived this as an insult, as though they were not real people, as though the Belgians were favoring the villagers by taxing them alone. I have known Mbuti to make the trek to the administrative post with money (begged or stolen or bartered from villagers) and insist on being allowed to pay taxes just like anyone else. All of a sudden the relationship took on a hierarchical aspect it did not have before. And the more the Mbuti resented what they took to be preferential treatment of the villagers, and the more they resisted the increasing demands on their services as laborers, the more the villagers sought to establish and confirm their superordination. Since for so long the villagers had remained ignorant of the forest world all around them, there was no way they could pursue the Mbuti into that forest and compel them to do their bidding, so they sought to coerce the Mbuti through supernatural control. Even the village assumption of western garb and certain western manners and customs was a way of increasing their supernatural power, rather than any concession to colonialism.

We shall discuss the major means by which the villagers sought to control the Mbuti, through the *nkumbi* initiation, a little later. For the moment it is enough to be aware that the villagers believed, with a disturbing intensity, in the existence of supernatural forces all around them, some of which were hostile (those associated with the forest) and some of which were friendly (ancestral spirits). In order to survive, the villagers had to manipulate these forces and bend them to their will. Sickness and accidental injury were always considered evidence of such forces at work. So when Mbuti failed to do the bidding of their *kpara* ("Patron" rather than "master," a term sometimes used) and fell ill, as they invariably did if they stayed too long in the village, then the villagers saw this as evidence of the success of their efforts to assert supernatural control over the Mbuti. Not believing in or practicing witchcraft or sorcery themselves, the Mbuti believed otherwise. Nonetheless there was a touch of ambivalence in their attitude, and regardless of the cause of sickness and misfortune, it increasingly became their experience that, for them, the village world was a place where things go wrong.

ISOLATION AND FRAGMENTATION

While tribal culture persisted despite the process of fission that characterized the immigration of all these villagers, the isolation of one village from the next, and the feeling of "difference," was clearly manifest in this dominating concern with control of the supernatural. Each village had its own distinctive character and mood. Some were as unfriendly and threatening as they looked, built as though the road running through the middle just did not exist. Others were built on one side of the road only, as though shunning all strangers while at the same time keeping their distance from the surrounding forest. Some were open, arid, and dusty—except during the heavy rains, when they became quagmires. Others were closed and more shady, but these were generally even less welcoming to visitors. Some villages took a delight in letting the road deteriorate on either side, and some were renowned for actually digging holes and trenches across the road deliberately to trap visitors from the outside world, virtually holding them at ransom until all their exploitable wealth had been exhausted.

In some villages this was more in the form of high-spirited fun, and indeed it *could* be fun to be held up in this way, though you generally paid dearly for it. In other villages it was more in the nature of active hostility. I have known all help refused those stranded in this way, and there are many stories of mysterious disappearances and deaths, though I was never able to document a single one. A few villages offered a warm and friendly welcome to visitors, though even there, and even in the smallest of villages, there would always be some who voiced

The Bira village farmers usually clear the forest so extensively that their villages have no shade, becoming hot, dusty, and unhealthy. Only the baraza *offers shade.*

suspicions that the visitor was in truth some malevolent force seeking to destroy the village. And against all those who passed through, on foot or by car or truck, most houses had medicine hanging from the eaves to ward off the evil carried by "others," even kin from a nearby village.

The larger villages, consisting perhaps of thirty or so houses, showed the same manifestation of suspicion and concern with supernatural forces within themselves. Families, lineages, and clans clustered together in clearly recognizable units, each with its own meeting place, or *baraza*, each with its own protective medicine. And as often as not, a single house could be found isolated on the outskirts of the village, or, sometimes, boldly established in its own special space right in the middle of the village. In the latter case it was most likely a blacksmith, always associated with the power to manipulate supernatural forces. Those isolated on the edges of a village were generally considered witches or sorcerers, though in the first instance they may actually have chosen to build their house there because they had no close kin or friends in that village. Even that in itself would be suspect, as would any preference for privacy.

Just as each tribe considered neighboring tribes to be masters of the craft of evil, accusing them of all manner of barbarity, including cannibalism, so each village suspected the next, and each household its neighbor. But it should not be thought that life was lived in constant fear and suspicion. The tendency to isolation took care of that. Just as each village was effectively autonomous and independent, politically and economically, so each family within a village took care of virtually all its own needs. The *barazas* were the only places where socialization took place, although outside the village there was always some socialization under a palm tree when it was cut for wine.

Palm wine cutting and drinking was serious business, however pleasurable. It was beneath the palm tree or when drinking wine in the *baraza* that disputes were settled and problems resolved, curses lifted and curses placed. It was here that you would find the real leaders of the community, not in front of the house of the government-appointed chief in one of the centrally located villages.

POWER AND AUTHORITY

At the village level, each married male was the head of his own household, though his wife had very specific rights and property. Within any one cluster of households, an adult male of the senior branch of that lineage would have more authority than the others and generally would speak for them in the event of some dispute. Over the village as a whole, a member of the founding lineage, even if a minority, would have special authority related to land usage. But that would be balanced by the authority of the "father of the *nkumbi*," an elective post associated with the initiation, which was held every three years, with the "father" likely to change on each occasion. The blacksmith had power rather than authority (as did those suspected of being witches or sorcerers). Since it was believed that he could manipulate the supernatural at will, his good opinion was actively sought and his ideas listened to with respect.

Similarly, over a group of several villages there was likely to be the power of a great ritual doctor, one whose role was reinforced with each successive *nkumbi* initiation. He could not only manipulate the lesser supernatural forces, but also had the power to invoke the ancestral spirits. And unlike the blacksmith he was honored at all times as being unequivocally on the side of "right," as working for the good of society, as upholding "the way of the ancestors." Many is the time I have seen the ritual doctor consulted by the government-appointed chief when the latter was totally unable to get his way with the recalcitrant villagers. In those days, despite the very real presence of colonial power, traditional beliefs and values, and the traditional power structure, were still supreme.

And finally, at the very apex, was the shadowy figure of a prophet. Prophets come and go in Ituri society. It was not a role filled in accordance with either heredity or skill, or charisma of any kind. Prophets arose in times of need, and the only requisite other than that need was that the prophet figure be in his person or his manner of being a clear manifestation of supernatural power. As elsewhere, this sometimes meant that the prophet was an oddball, even a former outcast. Invariably he was a solitary, living in seclusion. He did not need any skills of any kind; since he was believed to be a living manifestation of supernatural power all he had to do was to come into sight and the villagers were immediately on their best behavior.

I knew one such prophet well. His name was Mandevu, "the bearded one." I knew Mandevu over a period of a quarter of a century. He was as powerful when I first knew him as when he died, and he was always the same quiet, gentle, caring, good, simple man. Perhaps those qualities were what singled him out for the role. He seemed untouched by the mutual suspicion that existed between families and villages. He was one of the very few villagers I knew who was always serene, untroubled, unworried. It was indeed as though he was endowed with some special power.

Once, when I was very ill, I came out of a coma to find him sitting at the foot of my bed. He said something about the spirits of the ancestors walking across my chest. Then he just sat and stared at me with unblinking eyes until I drifted off to sleep. When I woke up some hours later, he was gone and I was on my way to recovery.

His first wife had died not long after they were married. Mandevu then took an Mbuti wife, and this was another quality that singled him out as someone special, for through his wife he had access to the supernatural power of the forest as well as that which he could reach through his village ancestry. By his Mbuti wife he had one son, Katchelewa. I have known Katchelewa since he was an infant. He is at home in the forest just as he is in the village, and is already on the way to becoming a prophet, like his father.

The need that Mandevu filled was the need for the reaffirmation of some commonly held values at a time when the combined forces of colonialism, commercialism, and missionary endeavor were threatening to sweep away all that made life worthwhile for the villagers. The more critical the crisis became, as independence approached, and through the Simba revolution, the more powerful Mandevu became. People would gather around him to make decisions. He would say nothing, just watch and listen in his quiet way. And when the decision was made, although he had said nothing, people would say it was his.

THE PRETENSE OF SUBSERVIENCE

No matter what the character of any village was, and though the degree to which villagers attempted to control and exploit the Mbuti varied greatly, the forest world of the Mbuti remained constant. Only the stories they brought back about the upside-down world of the village varied. Some villages, however, were more attractive to the Mbuti. In fact, being on the losing end of a bargain in which they were the only ones in real economic need, most villagers went out of their way to placate the Mbuti, since they could not directly coerce them.

What the Mbuti liked best of all was a village that they took to be the best of the outside world, but with the least amount of pressure attached to it. There they put the classical joking relationship into action in a masterful way. Rather than bartering or trading, as villagers did, the Mbuti brought their *kpara* and *karé* ("brothers of the knife," village men with whom they had shared the *nkumbi* initiation) whatever they chose to bring by way of forest products, and did just as much work as they wanted to, in return helping themselves to whatever they wanted from their patrons' households or plantations. If the village was at a strategic point along the road, there might be a small local "hotel" for truck drivers to stay overnight, or a store selling a few trade goods, including cigarettes, and another selling beer. The Mbuti played their games there as well, finding as much pleasure in the situation when an irate villager refused to give them any more

The larger villages offer various incentives to the Mbuti, encouraging them to bring in forest products in exchange for village products or trade items such as dried fish from the great lakes.

beer and tried to chase them along the road as when a less determined villager gave way and let them have whatever they wanted.

In such villages they could seem totally decultured, almost degenerate. They wore tattered and dirty western clothes cast off by villagers, many sizes too big, but worn with a certain flair that only other Mbuti seemed to notice, gently persisting in their constant ridicule of this nonforest world. They pretended to subservience, demanded idiotic sums of payment for work badly done, and complained long and loud about ill treatment. This all created among villagers (and travelers, including anthropologists) the illusion that the villagers really did have control, and that the *kpara* really were "masters." However, since their nomadic life demanded the minimum of personal possessions, whenever the Mbuti, singly or in any number, decided to abandon the village and return to their hunting camp, they could get their few belongings together and be on their way in a matter of minutes, with the frustrated villagers pursuing them to the very edge of the plantations, where the forest world began and the village world ended.

There is no doubt that colonialism, through the introduction of new ways of living, new forms of dress, a new technology and new material culture made the village world that much more amusing for the Mbuti to visit. Villages that could offer more than others by way of such entertainment tended to attract more Mbuti and hold them there for longer stretches of time, one week being a usual maximum.

Another way in which colonialism affected village life was by creating a need for specialized trades. Until then almost every villager had been able to satisfy his or her own needs within the confines of the nuclear family. A simple rotating market system now evolved, however, in response to the new economic demands made by the colonial administration. Markets were held at different villages on a rotating basis. Such villages became trade centers as well, where specialists such as tailors, hotel and restaurant keepers, store keepers, and scribes plied their trades. Some villages began to specialize in growing one kind of food and not another, where before they had grown both, so that the markets also became places where exchange of such staples could take place. An unforeseen consequence of this was that the barriers of mistrust and suspicion and self-sufficiency that had isolated villages from each other began to disappear. People found they could eat food and drink palm wine grown and prepared by "others" without getting sick. Even tribal boundaries were crossed in this way.

And of course every market place, on market day, was filled with exuberant Mbuti enjoying themselves at the expense of everyone else. It was as though they owned the forest and had allowed all these foreigners to settle there, and consequently could do as they liked. They knew how to play the game to perfection, seldom pushing the villagers to the breaking point, always conceding just enough and giving the villagers just enough of the vital forest products to keep them minimally satisfied. This side of the relationship was seen at the markets, informally, when most village marketers offered any Mbuti a sample of their goods (mainly food and drink) free. More formally, but less conspicuously, most villagers also ritually offered the Mbuti a token gift of the first fruits of their plantations.

ASSOCIATIONS AND FUSION

Markets became increasingly important as a means of expanding social horizons, linking village to village, tribe to tribe, villagers to Mbuti, and Africans to Europeans. But no mechanism served the forest as well in this respect as the *nkumbi* initiation, though the connection it made between African and European was negative rather than positive, since the Europeans opposed it vigorously. Missionaries opposed it as heathen and barbaric, cruel and dangerous. Administrators opposed it not only because it took able-bodied men away from productive labor on the

The nkumbi initiation, held every three years, provides a regular opportunity for different villages and tribes to join together in a common ritual. Here the sacred makata xylophone is being played in the foreground by the men, while women from a nearby village begin to dance in the background.

road and in the fields, but because it also posed a direct challenge to colonial authority, fostering a "contrary" and "backward" return to tribalism. Later events, in post-colonial days, proved them very wrong, but at the time European opposition to the *nkumbi* was strong and unanimous.

The initiation persisted, however, and every three years the sacred drums were brought out, the *makata* sticks cut, and the ritual doctors began what was effectively the major revitalization rite that provided all villagers alike, regardless of tribal affiliation, a relatively uniform basis for moral behavior, making order without threat of physical coercion possible. At that time the *nkumbi* did not link quite all the tribes: There were still some Sudanic peoples in the northeastern sector of the Ituri that refused to circumcise. But elsewhere it joined all the villagers together in a common festival, asserting a wider unity than could ever be guessed at under normal circumstances.

The practice demanded intervillage cooperation through a variety of rules, such as the one that each of a minimum of four house poles for the initiation hut had to be set in the ground by a member of a different village. Thus, at least four villages had to join together in the initiation of their boys, boys between the ages of nine and eleven most often.

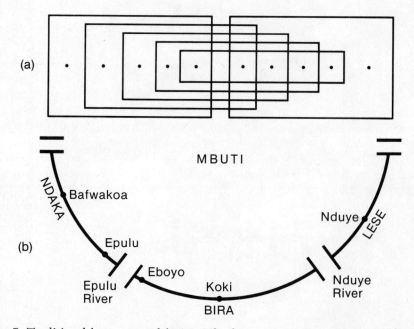

Fig. 7: Traditional forces toward fusion. The first section (a) represents overlapping political clusters, the broadening of social horizons within any one tribe and between tribes, brought about by traditional patterns of intermarriage, which correspond approximately to intervillage market and trade patterns.

The second section (b) represents the southern section of the nkumbi confederation, on which the boundaries of alliance in (a) above can be superimposed. The nkumbi, however, also incorporates the Mbuti.

Another rule was that Mbuti *had* to participate. The *nkumbi* could not be held in any village unless at least *some* Mbuti boys were available. This was for two stated reasons. One was to protect the initiation camp against malevolent forest spirits, who would not attack if their own people were there. The other was to create the vital *karé* bond between individual Mbuti and individual villagers. This was done, with typical village insistence on their own superiority, by cutting the Mbuti boy first "to clean the knife," then cutting a village boy with the same knife, so that their blood mingled. The two were then bound to each other for the rest of their lives in a bond that often was as affective as it was effective.

Thus in a very real way the Mbuti were the common medium through which all villagers throughout the forest were linked to each other, relating to each other differentially, but all relating to the Mbuti in the same way. Above all, as the villagers saw it, by putting the Mbuti through the village *nkumbi*, their most sacred ritual, consecrating young boys to the way of the village ancestors, they were placing the Mbuti under the direct control of those ancestors. No matter how much the Mbuti might ridicule the three-month-long ritual, and often their ridicule was open, if they completed the ritual then they were indeed subject to village supernatural sanctions.

To the outsider it often seems that the Mbuti can only be losers by their participation in the *nkumbi*; it seems that they have everything to lose and nothing to gain. But that is not so. The "need" that the Mbuti have for the *nkumbi* is, however, very different from that of the villagers in one respect. The villagers have economic need of Mbuti labor, skills, and forest products. The Mbuti have a political need—the need to keep the villagers from penetrating their hunting territories, which would surely happen if they did not supply the villagers with their material needs and provide them, as by their participation in the *nkumbi*, with at least the illusion of control. Even where economically possible, to ignore one's neighbors is to invite political disaster.

Even the Ngwana, the Muslim descendants of the Arab slave traders or of those who had sold their services to the Arabs, were members of the *nkumbi* confederation. If they had not been they would have been even more ostracized than they were, for the memory of slavery was still fresh, being far less than a hundred years old. Membership in the *nkumbi* was proudly displayed by the row of vertical lines tatooed around the chest, from front to back on both sides. This was done at the very end of the initiation, visible evidence of the boy-become-man's dedication to the way of the ancestors. Any adult male not bearing these cicatrizations was known to be an outsider, was not allowed anywhere near the *nkumbi* ritual, and was excluded from all important meetings and *barazas*.

On one occasion an *nkumbi* had opened, the initial dancing had gone on for a month to purify the village, and the first of a number of boys had been circumcised. Between each circumcision there was more dancing, and during one of these dances we noticed a Zande youth standing on a hillock, looking down at us. He was a worker at the nearby government national parks station, where he helped with the capture and training of elephants. The Zande did not circumcise, and he did not carry the marks of the *nkumbi*, so the ritual doctor sent a number of men to run and bring him to the central *baraza*. There it was decided that his uncircumcised presence had threatened the safety of the boys. The very presence of impurity, however unconscious, was a threat. The only way it could be countered was either by killing the offender or purifying him by entering him in the *nkumbi.*

Knowing the colonial hostility to the *nkumbi,* not to mention violence, the ritual doctor asked me what they should do. Just by being European I was inevitably associated with colonial power, if not with the administration itself. I gave the only answer I could, namely, that I was a foreigner, and that this was something that only they could decide. They then asked the youth, who was almost dead with fright. He was nearly six feet tall, and about eighteen years old. He said that he would rather enter the *nkumbi.*

He was immediately taken to the outskirts of the camp and the men shouted to the boys inside that another child was about to be "killed" and was coming to join them. Unlike the voluntary initiates, who are allowed to show their courage and strength by being circumcised either while standing or sitting on a trestle, this hefty youth was stretched out flat on the ground. I was made to sit on one leg while others sat on the rest of him to hold him down, and the ritual doctor, following all the prescribed steps and to the accompaniment of the sacred drums, slowly cut off the foreskin. It obviously hurt a great deal, and the youth struggled, but when it was over there was a look of something more than relief in his face. It was more a look of satisfaction.

As he was being daubed with white clay, to signify his death as a child, the men commented that "this is no Mbuti"—a reference to the fact that, whereas village children are taught never to show pain, least of all during the *nkumbi,* the Mbuti boys scream their heads off and run away if they can. To the villagers that is a sign of Mbuti inferiority, of their lack of "manliness." To the Mbuti it is merely good sense. If you are hurting it makes sense to say so, they say, and if the source of pain can be escaped then any sensible person should get away from it as fast as possible, for pain too is *akami,* and should be avoided. That is a typical example of how the values of the two peoples run almost in direct opposition, the same symbols meaning quite different things to each population. The very ritual that links them in an effective manner also separates them in the realm of values.

The Zande youth was then led into the camp and took his place among the diminutive preteenagers, as naked as they, and for the next three months was subject to all the same ordeals and deprivations, the butt of almost constant ridicule, all of which is carefully controlled by the ritual doctor so that no boy is given more to suffer than he can stand, while each boy individually is tested to the fullest and emerges with the satisfaction of knowing that he was on the brink of cracking but never did.

This episode provided a graphic example of how unimportant the small stature of the Mbuti is to their neighbors, and how mistakenly (from a sociological point of view) we place so much emphasis on it. How the Mbuti come to be short is as much a mystery as how some of their neighbors (including the Zande) come to be among the tallest people in the world. The Mbuti, at adulthood, may be anywhere between four and four and a half feet tall; four feet, two inches would be about "normal." The Zande youth in question was already nearly six feet tall. Yet despite the constant, functional, usually good-natured mutual ridicule, height is invariably ignored. Neither population sees any selective advantage in being either tall or short, and as yet makes no connection, as we so often do, between stature and status.

From the social anthropologist's point of view, the prime significance of the small stature of the Mbuti is that it renders them visibly distinct from all their neighbors. It thus creates an opposition that unites the culturally (and physically) divergent immigrant villagers in distinction from the highly homogeneous Mbuti. It emphasizes the already strongly recognized difference between the "children of the forest" and the newly-come immigrants. The maintenance of this distinction is an essential part of the overall social structure of the total forest population. The *nkumbi* is essential as a means for preventing the opposition, so visibly apparent, from degenerating into hostility and being threatened by isolation and ignorance. Above all, it provides an ideal opportunity for adolescents of each population to come to know each other and discover what they have in common by sharing this crucial moment in their lives.

The parents of the Zande youth came and thanked me for not interfering. They said that if I had done so, the villagers, out of fear of the colonial administration, would have let their son go, and later he would have been poisoned. As it was, he "graduated" with the rest of the boys. His parents were in the festive crowd gathered to celebrate the arrival of all these new men, fresh and pure from the very womb of manhood, the hope of the future. And, as it turned out, that youth was only one of the first of the Zande to enter the *nkumbi*.

ASSOCIATIONS AND FISSION

Of all traditional customs that the colonials sought to suppress, the *nkumbi* was the major one. But it flourished nonetheless, and went on to become a vital part of the new nation not yet born. They also sought to suppress the *anyota*, a sacred, but by no means secret, society of the Bali people, one totally mistaken by the Belgians to exist for the purpose of brutal slaughter and senseless cannibalism. Since members of the *anyota* carried distinctive scarifications across their stomachs and chests, resembling leopard claw marks, they were easily enough rounded up, and the Belgians proceeded to execute them all—all but a few of the youngest, whom they sent to mission schools for correction and conversion, and whom I later came to know.

Not surprisingly, they were among the most bitter of the critics of both colonialism and Christianity, for they knew the *anyota* for what it really was, a society to which only the most dedicated could belong, a society that existed to maintain and perpetuate all that was good and moral. At times it *did* involve members going into a trance, "becoming" leopards, and in that condition killing a victim and ritually consuming (just like a real leopard) a small part of the body. But such occasions were rare; they were moments of national crisis, when the future of the entire Bali nation was threatened by the failure of the people to live according to the "way." All were guilty to some extent, if not for sinning themselves, then for allowing others to sin, or for allowing conditions to persist in which the

The anyota, *or "leopard-man society," although outlawed by the Belgians, who executed its adult members, persisted throughout the colonial era, reappearing in other, much more overtly anticolonial forms allied to the dreaded* kitawala *society.*

ancient way *could* be broken. Usually only one or two people were killed on any such occasion (the most I was ever able to record from what old people remembered was six), and it happened only once or twice in a generation, they said. Those who were killed were not necessarily more or less guilty than anyone else, but they shared the guilt with all and were killed as a sacrifice.

That may be difficult for us to accept, but at least both the practice and the reasoning behind it are consistent with each other and openly dedicated to the good of the whole. It does not take much reflection to recognize that we follow much the same line of reasoning in justifying wars in which many more innocent people are killed, and we do not even make the excuse that those killed share the guilt with us.

The Mbuti, from their forest sanctuary, watched the hostility of the colonials to precisely those things that were most sacred to the villagers, like the *nkumbi* and the *anyota*, and more than ever took care to conceal from the outside world that which was most sacred to them: the *molimo*. They also saw colonial avarice in its exploitation of cheap or free (prison) labor on the coffee plantations and gold mines, where the mornings started, as I saw all too often, with a public flogging of workers who had not performed well the day before. And the Mbuti saw the Christian missionaries, most of whom sought to convert the Africans without even trying to understand the already extant and powerful belief in Spirit and Goodness, that is, the belief that there is a superhuman power that rules us all and that there is a moral, a right way of living. And seeing the lives of many of the missionaries, and the way they dominated and exploited even their converts, seeming to practice anything but the beliefs they preached, the Mbuti declared that they were not real people, and that their way was "empty."

The attitude of the villagers was less even-minded, less lacking in bitterness and hostility. The Mbuti could afford to be dispassionate. They still lived in the sanctuary of the vast inner forest and could shut the outside world away from their inner lives. For the villagers there was no such escape, and they saw all that was good to them being swept away. The few missions that were more true to the Christian message, like the few administrators who sought to rule with humanity, were not enough to avert the overall judgment of the village world, which was that the outside, colonial world was not merely to be opposed; it was to be destroyed.

CHANGE IN THE FIELD CONTEXT

In the last days before independence I could see the change in the attitude of the villagers towards myself, whereas my relationship with the Mbuti remained unchanged. At Epulu, a centrally located village that had been called Camp Putnam when I first visited it in 1951, Patrick Putnam had died in 1954. With him died the last reason for the villagers to respect the colonial world. For a quarter of a century Putnam had lived there, learning not one, but most of the local languages, while also learning about the beliefs and practices of those among whom he lived. Putnam had come to the Belgian Congo as an anthropologist, but he decided that since there could be no end to what he could learn, he would just stay. He set up a small hospital, and worked with the cooperation not only of the Belgian government, but also of the local traditional doctors. He used their herbal medicines wherever he found them effective, and always respected curative practices even when he did not at first understand them. He also ran a sort of "hotel." Actually he merely built two small cabins where overnight visitors could stay. Camp Putnam was the midpoint on the long road through the forest, and he simply offered the same hospitality that any African village would have offered, and just like the villages in this part of the Ituri he kept his visitors at a certain distance until he came to know them well enough to trust them, which was not often.

The villagers saw all this, and they respected Putnam for his primary concern for the good of the village society. Some Mbuti attached themselves to Putnam as their *kpara,* an event that he recalled with pleasure, as it led him to an understanding of how such transfers were effected between villagers. The compensation offered and demanded was a constant source of dispute, adding yet another factor to inter-village mistrust.

When Putnam died the villagers hoped that I would take his place. We looked somewhat alike, and it was assumed that we were kin, so I was classified as his son. He had become an integral part of the village world, a colleague of the great ritual doctor, Sabani, and a chosen companion of Mandevu himself. He was also a link between the village world and the colonial world, able to mediate, and thus keep the two worlds apart. When he died, all that died with him.

Not only was I expected to inherit his wives as my "mothers," and become the *kpara* to "his" Mbuti, I was also expected to receive visitors and keep them safely isolated from the rest of the village, and occasionally to entertain them with village and Mbuti music and dances so that the ever-increasingly necessary money could flow into the village. None of this, of course, could I do. For one thing, I was working with the Mbuti and was only in the village when they were, which was only for a few days every month or two. For another, as tempting as the prospect was, I could not see my way to settling permanently in the Ituri, giving my life to it as Putnam had done. And the less I had to do with the colonials and the missionaries the better *that* relationship worked out. My relationship with the villagers deteriorated rapidly, but that, if anything, merely improved my relation-ship with the Mbuti.

As Camp Putnam fell into disuse, since his third wife was unable to maintain it (although she gave it a good try), several other changes came to this part of the village world. A Belgian entrepreneur built an elaborate stone and brick hotel on the banks of the river, less a mile from where Camp Putnam, a secluded village of mud-walled houses, with Putnam's merely being rather larger than the others, still stood. Camp Putnam still thrived as a village, but there was no village around "Hotel David," and the villagers who worked there were all foreigners im-ported from other villages and other tribes. They were, as might be expected, not accepted into the village known as Camp Putnam, so they established their own on the roadside, as close to Hotel David as Monsieur David would allow (which was not very close). At the same time the government established a national park station for the capture and training of elephants, and the capture of okapi and other forest animals, some of which were to be kept there as a tourist attraction, and others sold to European and American zoos, providing some income from this rather unproductive region. Thus the village known as Epulu, from the river that flowed past its eastern fringe, was born.

Both the hotel and the *"station de chasse"* became colonial hang-outs, where Europeans disported themselves in ways hardly calculated to win the respect of the villagers. The Europeans, for the most part, did not realize how offensive they were being; they were simply too ignorant to be capable of such insight. On several occasions the villagers from old Camp Putnam begged me to intercede, since M. David was having them jailed if they refused to work for him, and the *station de chasse* was making equally impossible demands on them, sending them off to the notorious jail in Mambasa (the nearest administrative headquarters) if they did not "behave." In trying to intercede I do not think I came up against anything I would call evil, in the sense of conscious malevolence, but I did come up against a totally impenetrable wall of arrogance and ignorance. And this the villagers took to be evil, and this they knew they could only counter by invoking their ancestral spirits and, if possible, those of the forest.

ANTI-COLONIAL SENTIMENT

In the growing atmosphere of crisis it was clear that what was threatened was the forest as a whole, not just one part of it, and not just the villagers, nor just the Mbuti. This drew the Mbuti and the villagers closer together, and for the first time I heard the *molimo madé* enter the village at night, voicing its displeasure with the world at large. They still kept the villagers out of their sacred forest, but now at least they were allowing something of their sacred forest to enter the village and work its power in the profane world. Invariably, on the few occasions on which I was there when the *molimo madé* appeared, it directed its wrath in the direction of Hotel David.

As far as the work of the *station de chasse* was concerned, the Mbuti merely obstructed it in every way they could, giving false information about the movement of game in the forest, guiding would-be trackers and hunters in the wrong directions, and causing havoc in the compounds where the captured animals were kept.

The villagers equally disrupted the work of the hunting station as much as they could, though they paid a heavy penalty for this. Against Hotel David, which was an even more unnatural phenomenon (at least the buildings of the station were built in traditional village style, not of imported stone and brick), the villagers invoked the supernatural, laying curse after curse upon M. David, his family, and all who worked there. On one occasion the villagers had put a curse on me, partly because of my continued preference for the Mbuti and partly because I refused to accept my responsibility as Putnam's "son." It worked, and even though I knew it to be nothing more than psychological trickery, I became dangerously ill. Only the Mbuti rescued me by showing me how to combat the curse with one of my own—or rather by pretending to do so. So I could sympathize with M. David and his wife and daughter, as they suffered one malady after another. But I did not suggest a remedy to them, and neither did the Mbuti.

Even the initial rift between Camp Putnam and the new village of Epulu began to close. The villagers of Epulu, like the workers at Hotel David, had been imported from other parts of the forest. Many of them were Sudanic and did not circumcise, so they were not part of the *nkumbi* confederation, and not clean in the eyes of the local villagers. But in the last *nkumbi* before independence, workers from the station and from Hotel David were invited to participate. This decision was not made without opposition, for it was a fundamental departure from the most basic tenets of *nkumbi* belief in purity and the way of the ancestors.

In the discussions I noticed another remarkable departure from the norm: Although the Mbuti were still relegated to a totally subordinate role in the *nkumbi*, on this occasion they gathered in the men's *baraza* in numbers and vigorously argued that these foreign villagers should be included. After all, they said, *they* knew them, even if the local villagers did not, for didn't the Mbuti reach all the way through the forest, bringing forest foods and goods to all villagers equally? Some asserted, possibly with some truth, that they had visited Mbuti hunting territories on the far side and had taken Zande and Mamvu and others as their *kpara*, and had been treated by them just as "well" (they implied an exclamation mark after that comment!) as their own *kpara* within the *nkumbi*. The Mbuti argument carried weight, and it was a major innovation in the Mbuti/villager relationship that the Mbuti should even have been allowed to speak in the *baraza*. And so, in reaction to the growing crisis, the last breach in the *nkumbi* circle began to close. Mbuti and villagers moved closer together in common opposition to the colonial power, forest and village combining forces to oppose the outside world.

But whereas daily discussions in the *barazas* and under palm-wine trees became increasingly anti-European, talking of active resistance and ultimate assault against what was now perceived as consciously evil, in the forest the outside world was seldom mentioned. When it was, it was mainly by the youths, whose job it was to decide what changes were necessary in an ever-changing world. Their decision was that the Mbuti should spend more rather than less time in the villages, so that they could see what was going on and *then* decide what to do. The older men and women said that they had already seen enough, that the Europeans were even more bent on destroying the forest than the villagers, and could do so more effectively, with all their machines. But even they did not suggest active opposition; they merely counseled retreat, saying that the forest would look after its children.

In the village *barazas*, where (another change) women now gathered as well, the talk was not only of active opposition, but of violence. The defunct *anyota*, so senselessly eradicated by the Belgians, now emerged in a new, more truly violent form, under the name of *kitawala*. This was happening throughout the Congo, and in other places, springing in the same way from former institutions of social control that had been suppressed by the colonials. The *kitawala* was not an armed force of rebels. It was not even a revolutionary movement; it was an amorphous body of resentment and discontent. Its violence was more psychological than physical, but it paved the way for much of the violence that was to follow.

The *kitawala*, in keeping with the beliefs of the former sacred societies of this region, believed that in times of such enormous crisis the only solution was to appeal directly to the ancestors, normally unreachable, beyond the barrier set up by that puzzling phenomenon known as death. The *anyota* sought to pass through that barrier by assuming the guise of death, by becoming leopards, the symbol or harbinger of death, and then actually killing (presumably at the behest of the ancestors, for they never knew which of them had killed). In the same way, the *kitawala* sought guidance from beyond the grave, and identified with death, thus claiming access to supernatural powers that would more surely destroy the colonials than could any amount of physical force.

It was an uncomfortable time, to say the least, for the colonials. They knew that they were not merely resisted and disliked, but that they were hated and despised as unclean. The *nkumbi* took on new significance, and consciously defied all things

European, incorporating only certain European elements in a conscious attempt to gain supernatural mastery over an evil world.

On a couple of occasions I met Patrice Lumumba in Stanleyville, later to become Kisangani, the site of a major massacre of colonials. He was then the up-and-coming freedom fighter, and was beginning to spread word through the forest that the time was coming when all the villagers should rise up and drive out the Europeans, regardless of whether they were administrators, missionaries, or traders. He was talking of physical violence, and he was preparing for it, but he knew that this could only succeed if supported by the belief in supernatural warfare as well. We actually never talked politics; our only point of communication was music. But he spoke of the Putnams, and he named a very few other Americans and Europeans, including a couple of Roman Catholic missionaries and one Protestant. These he claimed had become Africans, and were no longer foreigners. This, for him, was the only way their inoffensive nature could be explained. Later I heard that I too had been included, as kin of Putnam, and would, with the others, be safe when the war broke out.

The forest was now full of talk of a war that would be greater than either that of the Arab slavers or that of Bula Matari himself. Although I never felt myself to be in danger, I felt unclean when in the village world, and shunned the company of other Europeans, for they were even more unclean. I began to notice, as did the villagers, that they smelled different, and this became so real that it made me nauseous to be near them. And certain of them, such as M. David and his daughter (but for some reason not so much so his wife), were even more offensive and more literally sickening than others.

I mention this because it is a simple fact. It says nothing and is intended to say nothing personal either about myself or those I mention. What it does say, or tries to say, is that in this time of perceived political crisis, resistance manifested itself in religious belief and practice, in an intensification of traditional values, rather than in what *we* would call effective action, such as strikes, physical violence, boycots, assassinations, and so forth. And in conjunction with this, perhaps even because of this, the peoples of the forest grew together as they never had done before, finding a point of agreement on what represented a common good, which they set against what they perceived to be a common evil: the colonial world that threatened all that made life worth living. I have been in other situations where the threat of physical violence was real, where I was in physical danger. Never was that nearly as frightening as the hostility I felt in the forest just before independence in the Belgian Congo, even though I was officially exonerated from blame and dissociated from "the enemy."

In those last few years the forest populations changed almost beyond recognition in their attitude toward the world around them and in their relationship with each other. As old barriers came down, new ones were set up. People talked of returning to the way of the ancestors, of going back to living the way they used to live, but it was plain that the world had changed forever and that nothing would ever be the same again. However much I regretted the good times that had passed, and dreaded what seemed bound to follow in the very near future, and however much I was dismayed and even disillusioned by the violence and hatred all around me, there came a strange excitement that was also a calm from knowing that this was how things had to be. I knew that it was right, whatever it was, just for that reason. And a ray of hope came from the knowledge that there were no master-minds trying to engineer the whole situation, that the situation was taking care of itself.

PART TWO | Independence

4/The years of war

THE NATURE AND PACE OF CHANGE

It might seem that the struggle for independence, the fact of independence, and the consequent realignment of political and economic values, themselves dramatic changes, would be responsible for increasing both the pace and scope of change in all areas of social organization. To some extent that is true, but it would be wrong to attribute any one effect to any one cause. The process of change is as complex as it is dynamic and all-pervasive, and illustrates convincingly the notion that all aspects of social organization are inextricably interrelated. But even more important perhaps, such reasoning draws attention away from the fact that, just as revolution is a different phenomenon from rebellion, so is change a different phenomenon from adaptation. Unfortunately we use the word *change* to mean several different kinds of transformation.

The pace and scope of change both began to increase dramatically long before the first manifestations of a conscious movement towards independence. The first and major cause was the invasion of the forest by Sudanic- and Bantu-speaking populations, bringing with them new ways of living and new ways of thinking. This happened, as far as we can tell, within the last four hundred years. It was heightened by the subsequent advent of the slave traders, the armed and often brutal incursions of H. M. Stanley, and finally, the arrival of Belgian colonialism, which not only induced change, but imposed it. But the nature of the change was still essentially growth, development, and adaptation. Continuity with the past was maintained in the Ituri by both the Mbuti hunter-gatherers and their village neighbors. The lack of readily exploitable economic wealth in the forest and the resultant *"laissez faire"* policy of the Belgians contributed to this.

But this gave way to a more aggressive colonial policy as the technology for effective exploitation became available. Then the pace of change increased to a point that adaptation was no longer able to meet the needs of the changing context. We then get the emergence of a series of what might be called social mutations, in which continuity with the past was abruptly severed, a distinctively new form emerging from the old.

One of the problems was that the Belgian colonials for the most part saw the problem exclusively in political and economic terms. They sought to incorporate the population of the Ituri, hunters and farmers alike, into the political and

*ave-
-alone*

the government "

81

In a typical roadside village camp just before independence, Mbuti sit in a roofless baraza *and discuss how they should respond to increasing demands for them to abandon the forest and become farmers.*

economic framework that was their paramount consideration. Only a year before independence some administrators were still talking of a "fifteen-year" plan, while the less optimistic had reduced their horizons to ten years. What now seem like insane attempts to effect political and economic transformation overnight were put into effect. More than once I saw administrators attempt to convert the Mbuti hunters into farmers, thinking they could do so merely by explaining the basic principles and providing the necessary materials, tools, and incentives. It never seemed to cross their minds that the Mbuti might have a completely different concept of time and space, and utterly different priorities in relationship to the world as *they* saw it.

Administrators watched indulgently as Mbuti responded to the lure of free food, clothing, housing, and other material benefits. Flocking out of the forest to the previously established "model pygmy farms," they took the seeds, followed the lead of their instructors, and dutifully planted them. The experiment did not last long, however. In cases that I saw it lasted little more than overnight, for as soon as the administrators and instructors withdrew at dusk, the Mbuti went out to the fields again, dug up all the seeds, cooked and ate them. It was beyond their comprehension why anyone should keep food sitting around for months before eating it, when all their experience told them that there is an abundance of fresh food available each new day. It was also difficult, if not impossible within their manner of perceiving time and space, to plan to be anywhere specific at any time that far into the future. After all, the Mbuti system of counting clearly indicates something about their needs: "one, two, three, four, many." And an Mbuti proverb, "If it is not here and now then it is of no significance," tells us, in their own words, even more.

But the Mbuti, at this critical moment in their history, still had recourse to the refuge of their forest home. Once again they had responded to external signals by coming out and experimenting, testing that which was new in the outside, nonforest world. Finding it lacking they simply went back to the forest and resumed their traditional pattern of nomadic hunting and gathering.

The villagers had no such recourse, however, and it was through *their* response to these new developments that, ultimately, the Mbuti also were affected. The colonial administration extended its influence through the government-appointed chiefs, so that all but the smallest villages were under direct supervision. The objective was as much economic as political, but that is not how it was perceived, since the villagers clearly were not going to reap much of the benefit. Further, as greater encouragement was given to European coffee planters and gold miners in the eastern part of the forest, so was greater injustice and indignity felt by the villagers, both those who worked (often as forced labor) for the Europeans and those who were compelled to cultivate their "own" cotton fields but who reaped little reward. (This was true even though at one time the Belgian Congo was Africa's third largest cotton producer.)

TOURISM, MISSIONS, AND REVITALIZATION

Still, since with Mbuti help the villagers could continue to raise their traditional crops they were still able to live to some extent in their traditional manner. What was really new to them, the most dramatic change from their point of view, was the way in which they were treated as inferior, almost subhuman. They saw these Europeans treating domestic pets with more consideration than they treated their African workers. A major agent fostering this resentment of perceived indignity was the growing hotel industry. This industry existed not so much for the benefit of tourists, though tourism was now beginning to become a potential source of revenue, but rather for the growing number of European administrators and settlers.

At Epulu, for instance, Camp Putnam had more than sufficed for the occasional European traveler, though for many it was far too "primitive" and they simply passed it by. It was (all but the tiny hospital that Putnam ran) an integral part of a very traditional village, with Putnam himself occupying much the same role as an African government-appointed chief (though without the disfavor that usually accompanied that position). Just before independence, however, Epulu took on added importance because of its central location, and the Belgians increased their official presence there by enlarging the animal-capturing station. Epulu thus became a government post with an armed "constabulary" and a team of European veterinary and zoological specialists. It also attracted foreign researchers and colonials looking for somewhere within the colony where they could vacation.

When Patrick Putnam died, and the "Hotel David" was built, Epulu became a place where, unwittingly, Europeans displayed themselves at their worst. In the midst of an essentially egalitarian society with little traditional distinction in wealth or power, they introduced those distinctions both among each other and between themselves and the Africans. Some of the indignities the Africans were made to suffer were unintentional, such as making traditional Arab dress, much as had been worn by the slave traders, the compulsory "uniform" to be worn by African domestic staff in hotels or the private homes of colonial administrators. Such staff was often also compelled to go barefoot, for it to seem all the more "authentic" to tourists. And, of course, regardless of their age they were referred to as "boy." Other indignities were very intentional indeed. Traditional beliefs were openly ridiculed, as was traditional authority. Sacred objects were pilfered and used to decorate profane walls or tables in colonial houses. Heads of families were publicly ridiculed as ignorant savages in front of their children, just as traditional leaders, political and religious, were treated like children in front of those who owed them honor and reverence.

The last vestige of whatever respect the Africans might have had for this foreign way of life was finally extinguished by the equally blatant disrespect of the colonials for their *own* stated code of behavior. I never once, for instance, saw a Belgian colonial beat a dog as viciously as all too often I saw them beat Africans, having made them expose their bare buttocks first and compelled their fellows to watch. And while they preached discipline and morality, the ranks of the colonials some-times seemed dedicated to the reverse. Juniors ignored orders of their seniors. Husbands sent their wives and children away so that they could maintain an African ménage, or even flaunted their mistresses in front of their families.

As if in response, one of the "mutations" I referred to suddenly appeared directly across the bridge over the Epulu river. At the side of the road there, as it rose up from the river banks, and looking directly across to the Hotel David, the Africans established a brothel, which they also called a "Hotel."

As they saw their own traditional values being threatened or attacked, the villagers reacted either by reinforcing their old beliefs or by replacing them, justifying new behavior by new beliefs. Adaptation was no longer possible. We could examine the role of hotels alone, in this context, and fill a book. But just one more example will have to suffice. As more colonials began to take vacations in the Congo, and as it became more possible for wealthy foreign tourists to visit the colony, the Ituri hotel industry blossomed. It began to cater to those more in search of entertainment rather than just board and lodging. There were two major attractions that the Ituri had to offer, pygmies and animals, probably in that order of importance, except that animals were easier to manipulate for entertainment purposes than pygmies. Epulu was an ideal site for both, and immediately prior to independence it was being developed for that purpose. But perhaps more scenically spectacular was Mount Hoyo to the east, almost in the foothills of the Ruwenzori and easier to reach for tourists from Uganda. Here an entrepreneur developed a whole pygmy industry. He invented "pygmy" dances, performed, of all things, in caves (places shunned by pygmies), heightened by the use of phosphorous and black light and anything else that modern technology could devise to show not just lack of understanding but contempt, so the Africans took it, for traditional beliefs and values. For dance, for the Mbuti and villagers alike, is sacred, and directly tied to the belief system.

Again, the Mbuti could always escape to the forest, and they took care never to dance their sacred dances in front of foreigners, so they were relatively untouched. For them it was as much a vacation as it was for the tourists; both enjoyed each other. But the villagers found themselves doubly insulted and assaulted. Whereas signs appeared up and down the road inviting tourists (colonial and otherwise) to come and see either animals or pygmies, there were no signs suggesting that anyone pay any attention to the villagers. There was a sudden deterioration in the formerly amicable relationship between the two populations. A few villagers tried to sell their own village culture as suitable for tourist consumption, but the few things that seemed to sell were all too often, like dance, those things that were sacred. Ritual objects sold much better, for instance, than ordinary arts and crafts. In this the villagers perceived again a frontal attack on the very essence of their being; and even when they rejected the temptation to sell that which was sacred, by contemplating it alone they were desecrated.

So while the Belgian administration was perceiving the growing agitation for independence as being political and economic, its foundations were rather in the destruction of traditional belief and practice, unwittingly and, often enough, with conscious deliberation. At the same time the missions in this area extended their activities and redoubled their overt efforts to destroy indigenous beliefs and practices. This was particularly true of the Protestant missions, which mostly shared the attitude expressed to me very clearly by one missionary. He had lived in the Ituri for nearly thirty years, and so it seemed reasonable for me to ask him about what he had learned of traditional religious beliefs in that time. His answer was direct: "Nothing, it is all evil." He was unable to explain how he could say something was evil when by his own admission he knew nothing about it.

For him it was an act of faith, but for Africans it was an arrogance and willful ignorance that could only be aimed at their destruction. The distance at which these missionaries kept themselves, both physically and emotionally, from even those Africans they managed to convert, and the way in which they exploited them for their labor, confirmed the feeling among the villagers that the missions were a major part of the colonial plot to destroy them. And the Africans considered them by far the most dangerous part, since the missions clearly were bent on depriving them of their very humanity. Given the central structural, ideological role of the nkumbi initiation, functioning as it did to help eliminate intergroup hostilities and frictions while promoting a powerful moral code acceptable to all, the combined opposition of the administration and the missions was more than enough to confirm this impression.

The Roman Catholic missions, which took a rather more intelligent and intellectual approach to the work of conversion, chose rather to build on what they already found by way of religious belief. They sought conversion through adaptation, rather than the mutation the Protestants seemed to demand. Some, like a couple of Jesuits I knew, felt that their own example was more important than any attempt to convert, and lived accordingly. Father Longo, at Nduye, while he sought (and by his own example won) converts among the villagers, refused to attempt to convert any Mbuti because, having been unafraid to learn during *his* thirty years in the forest, he had discovered that in the Mbuti language there was no word for "evil." In order to convert them, then, he would first have to teach them the concept of evil, and that he was not prepared to do. Unfortunately, the few such men and women to be found among Catholics or Protestants were not sufficient to dispel the growing conviction that the main threat to all Africans in the Ituri was not political repression or economic exploitation. Rather, it was the broad-fronted attack, both covert and overt, upon their very humanity, which rested in their concepts of self and spirit.

While liberationists such as Patrice Lumumba were busy creating economic and political awareness outside the forest, in the depths of the Ituri opposition took another form. Some said that it was the repressed "leopard man society," the *anyota*, that suddenly emerged in the Ituri under the name of *kitawala* (a name already connected with other forms of secret society elsewhere). I doubt that the correlation was either as narrow or as specific as that. It was rather that in response to the perceived threat to the very core of their being, the villagers, who could not find any refuge as could the Mbuti, fought Spirit with Spirit. The *kitawala* was associated by the colonials (as was the *anyota* formerly) with violence and murder. It was thought to be directed against them personally and aimed at their physical destruction, or at least their expulsion. Again they made the mistake of seeing only in terms of politics and economics.

In fact, the Ituri brand of *kitawala* was much more of a revitalization movement than it was a revolutionary movement. It was concerned with self rather than others, and with the spiritual self of the villagers rather than their physical welfare. It is not surprising then that it was a movement without members, for it was a body of belief rather than of practitioners. Much as with witchcraft, it is the belief rather than the practice that is the effective social force. There were those who for their own purposes claimed to be members of the movement, just as there were those who were so accused by the Belgians, but they were not the active principle. The beliefs that were the real revitalizing force were beliefs that established the village world of Spirit, the village supernatural, as superior to that of the colonial world in all its manifestations.

Thus there were beliefs that members of the *kitawala* could materialize checks and forge signatures so that banks would be compelled to pay out vast sums of money, which the *kitawala* would then dematerialize, in this way destroying the colonial economy. And there were beliefs that members of the *kitawala* had extraordinary physical powers and could leap over walls and even over whole buildings, thus making it impossible for the colonial police or military to pursue and capture them. Other beliefs attributed to the *kitawala* the power to become invisible (or sometimes "blue," which was associated with invisibility). This would enable them to be present at the most sacred rituals of the colonial "ritual doctors" (missionaries), to desecrate them without being detected, in this way subverting the greatest threat of all and confirming the supremacy of the village supernatural. Many were the reports we heard, almost daily, of such incidents actually taking place. Colonials increasingly huddled together by a log fire at the Hotel David and repeated such fantastic stories themselves, as if accepting some reality while pleading for a refutation that never came. Only in the depths of the forest, among the Mbuti, were the stories repeated loudly and openly with good-humored ridicule and disbelief. But repeated they were, and the disbelief was tinged with a certain amount of doubt; or perhaps it was only wishful thinking.

Each village was ready to list those in other villages who were members of the *kitawala*, but no one other than a very few eccentrics admitted to it. Those so named were always young men (and occasionally women) of irreproachable character. As with the *anyota*, it was believed that only the strongest and the purest, those most dedicated to the way of the ancestors, could bear the enormous responsibility and power that membership would convey. Like the *anyota*, then, the *kitawala* (in the Ituri at least) was seen by the Africans as a society devoted to the preservation of all that was right and good in the world, rather than a revolutionary movement devoted to the destruction of an enemy. Far more important than the emptying of colonial banks, or escape from pursuit, or even the desecration of what were taken to be hostile rituals, was the belief that the members of the *kitawala*, by their practices and self-sacrifice and moral dedication to the "way of the ancestors," invoked the presence of the ancestors themselves, *compelling* a return to the traditional ways.

As a matter of fact there was no significant increase in crime at this time that could not have been explained largely by the increasing disparity between the economic level of the African and European populations. But having themselves so successfully sown the seeds of discontent and revolution, the colonials saw it taking shape even in the most innocent changes of behavior. Similar were the desecration of a few churches, the tampering with or theft of communion wine and so forth. While some of this undoubtedly was part of a conscious attempt to undermine the ritual source of colonial power, or to obtain that power for the African cause, some of it was no more than a retaliation for the desecration of so much that was sacred to the Africans by the colonials. The number of those actively engaged in such activities remained fractional, and since the goal was seen by the others as compelling a return to tradition, anything that happened to the colonials was, in a way, incidental. And things that did happen were taken to be clearly the will of the ancestors.

From all of this the Mbuti were excluded, or excluded themselves, and since the bulk of the rest of the population equally took no part in subversive activity at first, this resulted in a deceptive appearance of continued subordination of the population to colonial will. The villagers knew that with the *kitawala* at work it was out of their hands and there was no need for further action on their part.

Those more politically active, mainly from towns and cities outside the forest, such as Bunia to the east and Stanleyville to the west, were not content to leave things in the hands of the ancestors. They made use of the *kitawala* phenomenon, however, and undertook a number of subversive acts, including acts of violence, in its name. Since everyone suspected everyone else of being a member of the *kitawala*, this gave the impression that the Ituri was full of active revolutionaries. These came to be associated by the Belgians with the political movement led by Patrice Lumumba.

When, after independence, Lumumba was assassinated, it was natural that his followers became the prime target for the heirs to political power. There ensued what has been called the Simba Revolution, the true story of which may never be known. It is certainly true that there were many years of bitter fighting up and down that once-peaceful, shaded road running right through the forest from east to west, and that there were massacres of civilians as well as military casualties. There are also more than enough well-documented incidents of rape, torture, and other physical violence and degradation practiced by both sides (though again virtually no evidence of direct Mbuti participation).

What is unclear is the extent to which the Simba actually believed themselves to have the powers attributed to the *kitawala*, and the extent to which they therefore saw themselves as having the same essentially nonviolent function of revitalizing traditional belief and restoring the way of the ancestors. There is enough evidence to suggest that this was true at least in part, just as it was true that some of the Simba were once political supporters of Lumumba, with political objectives, and others were villagers with little understanding of or interest in the political issues at stake.

All this badly needs to be explored if we are to understand the change that came to the Ituri as a result of the Simba Revolution, which effectively did not end until 1970. In the absence of reliable documentation, perhaps the best way for us to explore it is for me to repeat two accounts as they were given to me when I arrived back in the forest, in that year, just as an uneasy stability was beginning to return to the new nation of Zaïre. One account was given to me by a Bali villager, a fairly young man who had just been initiated into the *anyota* when the Belgians exterminated the society, allowing only a few of the youngest, including Buko, to live on the condition that they went to a mission school and became Christian. The other account comes from my old Mbuti friend, Teleabo Kengé. Needless to say, I cross-checked the stories as best I could with many others, and while I would not vouch for the literal or actual truth of events that are described, I believe the larger part of each story to be close to the truth. In any case, what is more important is the attitudes revealed, on the one hand emanating from the village world and on the other from the forest world. There is no question in my mind that these attitudes represent those held by a significant portion of both populations. As such they inform us more significantly than might any account, however accurate, that limited itself to what merely happened and ignored what was perceived to happen.

BUKO'S STORY

Even before the Belgians left we knew that there was not going to be an easy return to the old ways, to the ways of our ancestors. This was not because so many had taken up ways of the *wazungu* (foreigners). You knew me many years ago when I was a young man, without children, and you know how I used to be. I worked for the *wazungu*, wore their clothes and did their work, smoked their cigarettes and drank their beer. But I never gave them my heart; even when they hanged my brothers and fathers (in the *anyota*) they could not touch my heart. So wearing their clothes and eating their food, even going to their empty churches is not going to touch my heart, or that of any *real* person. The *kitawala* showed us all how powerless the *wazungu* are in the end, for the whites have no heart; all they have is physical power. The *kitawala* made sure that even that would be defeated, and it was thanks to the *kitawala* that independence came with so little violence.

But even before the *wazungu* left other strangers were coming in, from other parts of the country: black *wazungu*. After independence they wanted to control our lives, just as the white *wazungu* had done. Most of us did not mind that; we thought that we would keep the good things the *wazungu* had brought but go back to the old ways. But I was afraid, because I had already seen that, unlike the white *wazungu*, these new strangers *had* hearts, hearts that were as powerful as ours, but different. They had their own ways and respected them, but did not respect ours. They laughed at us and called us savages, just as the whites had done at first. And they laughed at our beliefs. That is something the whites never did. When the whites tried to destroy our beliefs it was because they knew that was where our strength lay. But these new *wazungu* were different, and I was afraid at first. When the years of war started, when Patriko [Lumumba] was killed, thousands of his people from outside the forest came in and tried to take control. When the new government sent in an army of white soldiers with guns and tanks and planes we knew that the Simba ["lions"], as they called themselves, were really *kitawala*, for although they only had bows and arrows they never got killed. And when we knew they were *kitawala*, we knew we were safe, for they had hearts like ours, these Simba.

In the first days of the war, before the tanks and planes arrived, the Simba came from village to village and asked us all for the names of those who had treated us well after independence, and those who had not given us respect as real people. And when we pointed to those who had not given us respect, like some of the black *wazungu* as well as most of the white, they simply killed them. But they killed them completely, not just once, as whites do, but three times. They shot them with their own white guns, cut their throats as the Ngwana cut the throats of animals, then tied their hands behind their backs so they could not swim and threw them into the river. Right here at Epulu all those who did not respect us were hiding in the Hotel David. That was the right place for them to die, and when they had died the hotel was killed too. There was never any evil here until that man came and built that place.

But the Simba were too powerful for him and those like him. The Simba use mirrors, like the *kitawala*. They can hold up a mirror and the evil that is in you will return and make you helpless. I have seen it. I saw the Simba, wearing nothing but bark cloth and carrying only bows and arrows, just like we used to do in the old times, times when we were real people, just walk down the middle of the road, from Musafili's old village; and in the middle of the day I saw them stand in a circle around the hotel. They had their backs to the *station de chasse*, they knew the soldiers there would not dare to bother them. The *wazungu* fired at them with their rifles and pistols, but not one Simba fell. That was when they started closing in on the hotel, from all sides, as I watched from my house—it was just where it is now, looking right down on the hotel.

And then they disappeared into the hotel and I could hear the *wazungu* crying and saying they had meant no harm, that they would do whatever was wanted of them, they would give the Simba all their wealth. Even then they did not understand that their wealth is nothing to us—that they are welcome to it, if that is all they want. And even then they could not bring themselves to respect us as real people. Hearing them cry like children made *me* feel unclean, and like a child, not a man. Real men do not cry. Hearing them made me feel weak, and then I realized this was their last weapon, their last attempt to defeat us by *mayele*.* But it did not work on the Simba. As they entered the hotel they became invisible, so the *wazungu* did not know where to cry to. That is why all the shooting stopped and there was only crying, as they tried to turn the Simba into children who had not seen the *nkumbi*, children who had not yet touched the way of the ancestors.

Then I heard more shots, and the crying stopped. The bodies of the *wazungu* were carried out and their throats were cut, their hands tied behind their backs, and they were all thrown into the Epulu to die again by drowning. Then the Simba went on to the next village, and so on until they got rid of all those with evil instead of hearts. And always they asked the villagers who was evil and who was not; they did not ask who was black and who was white. Everywhere they told us to return to our old ways and bring back the way of the ancestors. We knew then for sure that the Simba were good people. It was what *we* would have done [in the *anyota*].

But then, in came the white armies from the south [South African and other mercenaries] with tanks and planes. Since they could not see the Simba they just dropped bombs and shells everywhere. They destroyed every village, house by house. They never stopped to ask us who was good or who was bad, or what we wanted, and if we tried to stay in our houses or fields they just killed us. There was nothing to do but run away into the forest. All of us. There was not a villager left along the whole road except a few Ngwana that the Simba had not killed; they were the only ones to stay when these newcomers came with their bombs and guns. Those were terrible days, because the deep forest is not our home. We lost our way and went hungry. I was with a few other men in my field when the tanks came into Epulu, and I knew from what I had heard then that there was nothing to do but run.

There were four of us. By nightfall there were only three; one had lost us on the trail. None of us knew where we were. We stayed awake all night in case we were attacked by forest spirits. In the early morning we hurried on, further away from the village, and we did not stop until late afternoon. We hoped to find something to eat, but we were afraid to eat the fruits and berries we saw, as we did not know whether they were safe. The Mbuti say that most of them, like the mushrooms, are poisonous. Only the water we could drink safely. Then we were afraid to go any further because we no longer knew in what direction the village lay, and we were afraid that the *saitani* (evil spirits) would lead us back there to be killed.

I think it was the third day when we were found by some Mbuti. I did not know any of them, none of them were mine or belonged to anyone from Epulu, though they said they knew Makubasi and Ekianga and some of the others of our Mbuti. They said they knew what had happened to all the villages, and that quite a lot of us who had tried to escape had died from exposure or hunger or from eating poisonous food, or had been killed by animals or *saitani*. They said they were sorry for us and invited us to come with them back to their hunting camp, so we did. There was nothing else we could do. That night they built us a house outside the camp, in a small clearing of its own, and said they would guard it for us. They brought us our food there, and gave us leaves to make a bed with.

And that is how we lived for seven years. More real people joined us, some from Epulu, some from other villages, even some from the other side of the

* *Mayele*: trickery—a nonhuman quality that can be cultivated by humans, or used by evil spirits masquerading as humans.

forest it seemed, because they were uncircumcised and unclean. Nobody knew where we were. But whenever the Mbuti moved we moved with them, and they always helped us build our own village near their camp, and brought us food for us to cook as we wanted. Sometimes we were able to stay in our forest village for several months, as long as it was close enough for our Mbuti to bring us what we needed. I am told that some people from Epulu managed to build a village right near the middle of the forest, where the Mbuti never hunt, and found a clearing in which they could grow some bananas and manioc they managed to get by stealing back into the village with the help of their Mbuti. But the Mbuti always stopped us from cutting down enough trees to make a real village or real fields. I have heard the same story at Eboyo, and of course old Kopu always had a secret plantation hidden way off in the forest where the Belgians could never find it. But we were not so lucky. Our Mbuti did not want to take us back to the road to get the bananas and manioc, and would not get them for us. They told us it was too dangerous. So we lived off the food they gave us, and did what we could to get more by setting some snares on the trails close to our village camp.

Life was hard. The food was not good, without bananas and manioc or rice it was tasteless. We were afraid to follow the Mbuti to learn what fruits and berries and roots they gathered for themselves, and how they knew what mushrooms were safe and which were poisonous, because like the *kitawala* they can become invisible. If they did that then we would have been lost again, and the forest was full of *saitani*. I never actually saw one, but they kept attacking us and making us ill, so we knew they were there. At one time our village camp had about twenty people living there; one of them I made my wife. But none of the children born survived, and by the time the years of war were over there were only ten of us left. My wife was one of those who died. The *saitani* caught her by her stomach and killed her. Others were caught in their bowels or in their chests. I nearly died several times.

We were defenseless because our way demands that we have the *nkumbi* festival every three years. We had already missed one, and now we missed two more because the *nkumbi* has to be held in real villages, and the *baganza* [initiates] have to eat real [village-grown] foods. If we had held an *nkumbi* there in the middle of the forest our boys would have grown into Mbuti, not into men. We had one boy in our forest village camp, the son of Vasan at Eboyo. You know him. He looks like a man now, but he is not, he is still uncircumcised. But now that we are back, out of the forest, you will see an *nkumbi* like you have never seen before. Our boys will become men, and we men will be made strong and good again, and with the *nkumbi*, now that there are no *wazungu* to stop it, the way of the ancestors *will* return.

KENGÉ'S STORY

This was told to me two or three months later, when I was finally able to find where Kengé had ended up, in the forest about fifty miles to the east of Epulu. I told him Buko's story, half expecting a snort of derision and total contradiction as well as ridicule. What follows combines his immediate response and some of the things he told me from time to time during the months to come.

Yes, those villagers had a bad time. It was bad for us too, because they left all their plantations and ran away, so very soon there were no fields for us to steal from. The Simba and soldiers had nothing worth stealing, they were *bulé* [empty, useless]. But it was the villagers' own fault. They let the *wazungu* touch them. When Putinam was still alive he refused to let the *wazungu* touch the villagers. He was like their chief. You saw how he used to work with old Sabani and Mandevu and the other powerful [ritual] doctors, and like them he cured sickness and kept the place good. But when he died and that David came to Epulu with his smelly daughter, the curing was over, there was no more making anything good, and the villagers gave up trying. They do not have a *molimo* to make everything good, and the *wazungu* nearly killed their *nkumbi*.

But the stupid villagers did not even seem to know what was happening to them. Buko may have thought it was wrong for them to imitate that David and build another house for women on the other side of the river, but most of them enjoyed it. At first we thought they were taking our *elima* [the Mbuti girl's premarital/puberty festival, where girls invite the boys of their choice to sleep with them, but under carefully controlled and socially approved conditions]. But then we saw they were using their women for mere sex, as though they were female elephants, and that the women were selling their bodies like they sell their manioc or bananas. Any people who do that are asking for trouble, asking to be killed.

By imitating the ways of the *wazungu* the villagers thought they could become *wazungu*. Even I would not drink their palm wine when I saw that, and I left Epulu and went far into the forest. Epulu had become a bad place to stay, a place of *akami* ["bad noise"]. I was not there when the Simba came, but I was at the village of Katala when the same Simba came on up the road. It was so funny to see how afraid the villagers were! Some of them fled into the forest even then, before the *wazungu* soldiers came. They thought the Simba were *kitawala* just because they wore bark clothes and carried bows and arrows, like us. But then those stupid people think we are spirits too, sometimes!

Of course the Simba were not *kitawala* . . . the *kitawala* never existed any more than evil spirits exist. Those things only exist in the mind of villagers. We Mbuti know better. As for Simba becoming invisible, or jumping over houses, or not being killed by bullets. *Mavi!* [literally, "shit"] Only *wazungu* and villagers could believe stories like that. But the Simba *did* kill *some* people three times. I saw that. But you had to be very bad to be killed three times, otherwise they only killed you once or twice and instead of giving you to the crocodiles gave you to the worms in the earth.

Buko is right about the way the *wazungu* cry when they die. I had never seen whites die before, except when Putinam died, but he was not really one of them. He died like a villager. The *wazungu* died like baby antelopes who don't know how to die, and wriggle and kick and gurgle and look frightened when they are dying, and go on making funny noises until all the spirit has left their body. But I don't think the *wazungu* had any spirit in them, only bad air. They smelled terrible as they died. No, the villagers are not real people, not really, but the *wazungu* were not even animals. I don't know what they were, but we were glad when they all went, and glad the Simba got rid of any who stayed. The good *wazungu* became villagers, like Putinam had done, and the Simba did not bother them.

After all the villagers fled to the forest there was nothing much to come down to the road for, but sometimes I did, just to see what was going on. I was not afraid, but I took care always to walk down the middle of the road. The *wazungu* soldiers always stepped aside as though they were afraid, and shouted at me. Perhaps like the villagers they thought I was a *saitani*. I don't know. I did not like them—they made too much noise and never laughed. I liked the Simba though. They drank lots of palm wine and used to share their food with me, though they were a little afraid of me too; I noticed they never touched me. And the only villagers they harmed were the black *wazungu*, Ngwana, and villagers the Belgians made into chiefs. But the Simba never stayed long enough

Many Mbuti told me much the same story as Kengé. Here two Mbuti men working for the game park point out the same place behind the Hotel David where the killing took place. Shortly after this photo was taken these two, dressed in bark cloth, quit their jobs and rejoined their forest hunting band.

to grow village foods and that was bad. Sometimes they came into the forest and we gave them food, and when the *wazungu* soldiers were trying to capture them we hid them and protected them.

We did that for the villagers too. After all, they are our *karé*; we have all seen the *nkumbi* together. We could not let them die. A lot of them *did* die, but not because they were killed. They died because they were too stupid to let us help them. Some of them thought they could get their own food in the forest, and of course they went and picked all the most poisonous foods and died as if they had army ants in their stomachs. They have no brains at all. Where I was we had a whole lot of them, almost a complete village. We let them cut a few trees down, though of course they wanted to cut the whole forest down so they could see the sky. That way they could build a village, and they lived there for most of the war. It was about three days away from the road, so they were quite safe, and we used to bring them all the food they needed. They managed to grow a few things, but not much. Some Mbuti let villagers cut down more trees so they could grow their bananas and manioc and rice and the Mbuti could steal them. But I think that was wrong. It is all right to cut down one or two trees, but even that is not really good. And we did not need the food. I think what we missed the most was having villages to steal from and villagers to make fun of.

Sometimes we visited in their forest villages, but they were so sad and often so sick that there was not much fun to be had there. And sometimes they came to visit us if we were nearby. Then it was as though their camp was our *bopi* [children's playground] and we quite liked having them to visit and play in *our* camp. They seemed less stupid when they were with us, and we had never seen that before because, of course, they never used to come into the forest, except a few strange ones like old Kaweki. So we let them come, but never let them build their houses or live in our camps. They could just come to play.

But in this way they saw things they had not seen before and began to ask us questions. In our camp I know quite a lot were there one night when the *molimo* came in to be fed at the *kumamolimo*. It did not seem wrong. The villagers thought it was a real forest animal they had never seen before, so they kept back. The *mangésé* [Mbuti elders] were angry at the youths for bringing in the *molimo* and singing while the villagers were there, but the youths said that the villagers were forest people now, and needed the *molimo* as much as we did. After all, they take us into their *nkumbi*; they have done so for years and years, and they are still alive. So while they are with us in the forest, should we not let them see the *molimo* just as we have seen the *nkumbi*?

Perhaps the *nkumbi* is not as *bulé* as we think. I am not sure, but I know we let the villagers see the *molimo*, though we never told them what it really was, or let them speak to it or ask it for anything. As I said, they were like children living in their *bopi*. But we *did* begin to let them sing like adults, even though they don't know how to sing. That is why now, sometimes, we bring our *molimo* out of the forest and into the village on the road, to help them. Life is still hard for them, even though all the white *wazungu* have gone. These black *wazungu* also ask for a lot from them. But we do *not* want them back in the forest again. They make too much noise all the time. And they still don't know how to sing.

We are much wiser now though; perhaps their coming to the forest was a good thing. Or perhaps I am becoming a *mangésé*, an elder, and am learning how to *think* things right. Anyway, the forest is not the same, but it is not because the villagers destroyed it like the elephants they are and like the old *mangésé* said they would. Tungana, Moké, Manyalibo, Masisi—they all said that if we let the villagers come and live with us it would kill the forest. They did not kill the forest, and I think some of them respect it, those who at least try to sing. But something happened, and the forest is not the same. And now the village is different too. I like the village world as much as ever. I like to smoke their cigarettes and drink their beer as well as their *bangi* [marijuana] and *mabondo* [palm wine], but I still think it is wrong when the youths bring the *molimo* into the village, as they sometimes do now.

I am no longer a youth; I am a father, so I cannot tell them what to do. I think that if I were really an elder I would remind them of how good things used to be when we kept the *molimo* deep in the forest—you remember, near the Lelo River? *Ai!* what a clean place that was. Somehow, since the villagers came to live in the forest there has never been the same *ekimi* [quiet, cleanliness], and the young people today actually seem to allow *akami* [noise, uncleanliness] into their lives. You ask them; you see if I am wrong. I know you think I tell you a lot of stories. But I am a father now. You ask them. Some of them don't even know what the words mean any more. When I try and tell my own son, Atoka, now that he is ready to see the *nkumbi*, he laughs at me and tells me I am so old that I am dead. I know I used to be like that too. But you have been to the Lelo, Mulefu, and you must know I am right. Atoka has never been there. Perhaps he and the others have never known *ekimi*. Perhaps we should all go back to the Lelo and sing like we used to.

5/The village world

LIMBO: WORLDS IN TRANSITION

For nearly eleven years I was unable to get back to the Ituri because of the political upheavals that followed independence. I had seen independence come to neighboring Uganda and Kenya, but that in no way prepared me for the change I *felt* on landing at Kinshasa in the early part of 1970. In both Uganda and Kenya, even at the worst of times, there was always some sense of direction, even though one direction succeeded another. Even in Kinshasa, the capital of Zaïre, however, it was almost as though it was the Mbuti who had taken control and imposed their nondirectional sense of time and space on the new nation. There was no sense of things "going backward," as the dispossessed colonials were quick to claim; but neither were they going forward. It was like being in a limbo world, neither African nor European, neither progressing nor regressing, yet strangely alive and vital.

My colleague and I took the river steamer to Kisangani, as Stanleyville had been renamed (and as the Africans had always called it). Day after day the steamer chugged against the current, the shoreline slipping past slowly, so that there was plenty of time to examine every detail and listen to every sound. It was indeed a timeless world. The only signs of modern civilization were the steamer itself and the outboard motors that some Africans had put on their huge canoes, hewn out of solid tree trunks with hand-forged axes and adzes. In ten days we saw only three settlements built in colonial style. Only at the very end of the journey, as Kisangani came into sight, was the reminder of colonial days unmistakable. Until then it was as though Buko's dream had come true, as though the whole of the new nation had returned to the way of the ancestors.

But at Kisangani the old "native" town, as ramshackle as ever, lay low on the south bank, while on the north bank the Roman Catholic cathedral reared upward from the very banks of the river, right above where the old colonial port buildings still stood. And behind them were the palm-lined streets and avenues leading to the Governor's Palace and other public buildings no less indicative of the European presence.

But within a few yards of the port gates it was clear that the presence, while still there, was now dead and decaying. It was as though the new independence had chosen to let the past die, and remember it only in decay, rather than attempt

95

to drive out all memory of what had once been so powerful. There was no monument to those, African or European, who had been massacred at various street corners. Yet it was as though it had happened yesterday, the feeling of death was so strong. Almost everyone I asked could point at once to a nearby spot where some act of violence had taken place. Not one of them tried to justify or condemn the violence; it belonged to the past. But it hovered in the air, a pervasive reminder of the days of war, and of the need to return to the way of the ancestors. Though only in the old market were you likely to see African males in traditional dress, and despite the grandeur of the old colonial buildings and the imposing presence of modernity in the form of newer buildings such as the Congo Palace Hotel, it was the presence of tradition that seemed to dominate.

But that was in the streets, not in the seats of power such as the new Governor's residence and the university. Here that power was quietly consolidating itself, preparing to do the will of the new national government halfway across the continent, down at Kinshasa. Here were the black *wazungu* that Buko feared almost more than the whites.

Within my first few days in Kisangani that new presence made itself felt, a curious, horrific, yet strangely hopeful blending of the old and the new. There was to be a public execution, and the governor had my colleague and I driven there, so that with the population of Kisangani, who were ordered to attend, we could learn about the new rule of law. The new government of President Mobutu was until that moment almost unknown in this part of the nation.

I had read the usual accounts of public executions in Africa, accounts describing them as savage spectacles or orgies of brutality, with crowds drinking and cheering. These accounts conform a little too readily to the image the western public seems to want, or need, of brutality in the nonwestern world, for me to give them much credence. And there are conflicting accounts. But on this one occasion something quite different took place. The horror was there, but it did not lie in the people, in the supposed savagery of the criminals, the executioners, or the assembled spectators, nor even in the law that required the spectacle. The horror lay in the chain of events that made such a spectacle virtually inevitable, if not necessary.

The trappings were distinctly European: a makeshift gallows, the two nooses dangling at the ready, the hoods waiting to be pulled over the faces of the criminals at the last moment, the governor in full panoply, waiting to read the sentence and give the order. But other elements, material, judicial, and emotional elements, were just as distinctively African. There were two chairs on the scaffold, for instance, for the criminals to sit on during what was obviously intended to be a long wait. They served to give the criminals the oportunity, which both took, to reject them and sit more comfortably on the floor, as though at home rather than on display. From there they looked down on us as we looked up at them, and there was no question that, to begin with at least, we (the public) were more nervous— in part embarrassed, in part ashamed, in part frightened—in a word, guilty.

Here was the traditional jural system at work, telling us that no man is totally bad, that no crime is committed by one man alone. I was reminded of how the Mbuti youths, when they carry the angry *molimo madé* into the hunting camp in the dead of night to punish those who are creating *akami* and destroying the hunt never merely assault the house of the major offenders, well known to all, but with enormous deliberation attack every single house in the camp. The guilt and the punishment are shared by all. Here only two were to be punished, but we were all made to feel guilty as they looked down on us, as though they were the judges and we the condemned.

Then when the governor, perhaps feeling that we had been punished enough and made to recognize adequately our own imperfections and guilt, gave the signal, each man in turn was given a bull horn and allowed to address the crowd. Now the roles shifted subtly. One of the men, sensing that the end was near, collapsed on the floor and from there could barely whisper that he had nothing to say. His companion, however, spoke to us for what seemed like an eternity, in a loud, clear, and almost friendly voice, as though talking to his family. Both were Simba "rebels" who had refused Mobutu's offer of amnesty, having learned the hard way, under Tshombe, how unreliable a thing the amnesty of black *wazungu* could be. Those who had accepted had found Mobutu to be true to his word. But he was also true to his word when his repeated offers of amnesty ran out, and those who refused to the end were hanged when caught.

Sitting calmly on the floor of the scaffold, almost directly under the noose that was to choke him to death, the second Simba told us all this, and admitted that he had in the end killed innocent people in order to survive while avoiding pursuit. But he also told us that the prior and greater crime was to have denied the law of the new nation, under Mobutu, so that it was a crime against the nation rather than against those he had killed, and for that he deserved to die. Nonetheless he recognized the harm he had done to individuals, to their families, and to all of us, as if including us in his personal grand-family. He ended by thanking us for allowing him to acknowledge his guilt openly to so many of those he had offended, and thanked us for coming to make his death good.

I think it was at that point that a steady drizzle started to fall, and I found my knees shaking uncontrollably. I saw that others were equally moved. The guilt had been taken from us, but now we were forced to share the role of executioner. When it was all done, something very African, in keeping with so much of the local tradition, had happened. I was to remember this moment when Buko talked of the way the *anyota* sometimes had to kill, even good people, to preserve the nation, and that such people died honorably for the good of their friends and family, to preserve the way of the ancestors. Justice had been effected in a very African way, even using the procedures and trappings of the colonial world left behind and of the western world that Zaïre now had to face. The guilt had been dispersed and disposed of rather than being meticulously allocated and preserved in the criminal record. Instead of retribution there had been restitution, Honor had been restored to those whose lives were taken, and hence to their families who had to survive and continue in the world of the living. And "the way," which might be translated as "social order," had been restored to the community in the name of the nation.

Unfortunately, this last benefit of such traditional rituals, the linking of the good of the individual to that of the community in particular, and the widest political entity in general, could only be nominal. The new political unit called the Republic of Zaïre was still beyond the comprehension of most, even in a major provincial capital like Kisangani. It was recognized and accepted, but not known and understood. Yet the execution, done in the way it was, served to *begin* to bring the nation into the local context by suggesting that it was not something entirely unfamiliar and, not like previous governments, hostile to all tradition. In the next few months the work of adaptation was to continue right through the forest, with tradition playing a major role, not in isolating this remote and hitherto neglected part of Zaïre from the rest of the nation, but rather in helping to incorporate it fully and firmly. That process of adaptation was to continue as long as the good of the nation was the paramount concern, and was to diminish as private interests, commercial or political, superceded public concern.

The need for the widest kind of public unity was demonstrated everywhere. As we left Kisangani for the heart of the Ituri, it was most immediately evident in the almost impassable condition of the road, as well as in the devastation of the countryside on each side. It was along this road, part of a system that virtually encircled the forest, that the village world had been established, the villages thus being distributed in a strictly linear fashion rather than grouped in clusters. And the road, which had originally been a foot trail, then was expanded by the Arab slavers and Stanley into a major forest pathway, and ultimately by the colonials into a motorable highway, had always been the major, if not the only, avenue of communication between villages. In this way, villages at each extreme end of every tribal territory had more communication with villages of the adjacent tribe than they did with each other. And only by the road did the forest population have any communication with the outside world. With the road gone, communication was at a standstill.

There were still, at this moment, quite a large number of Simba still in the forest. Like those we had just seen being executed, they killed in order to stay alive, so that nobody who saw them could report their presence. The condition of the road meant that, in any case, any kind of police action was necessarily confined to wherever there were police at that moment. It did not diminish our sense of insecurity to find that we had to travel a hundred and sixty miles, averaging something like ten miles an hour, before coming across anything resembling police, soldiers, or other representatives of the rule of law. In fact, throughout that entire distance, once beyond the outskirts of Kisangani, there was little sign of any human life at all. Where there had once been villages every few kilometers, there were now long stretches without as much as a single house. There were only two or three villages as such on the actual roadside.

ENVIRONMENTAL CHANGE

Another drastic change that had taken place since I had last traveled the road, eleven years earlier, was that the forest had been cleared on either side for sometimes as much as a mile, creating an open strip averaging a mile wide through the middle of the forest. And it was the same beyond the military post of Bafwasende. There the trees used to meet, or almost meet, high above the road, the sky only truly becoming visible when one entered the vicinity of a village, where the forest

The road through the forest has been widened so that it no longer even resembles what it was in the colonial era at the same place (see photo, page 26). It is impossible yet to estimate the damage to the fragile ecology.

had been cleared for plantations. What had happened was that in the last days of colonial rule and through successive governments, for economic and military/political purposes, the once-narrow dirt road had been doubled in width. And to maintain it cantonments had been established for the roadworkers. This not only increased the number of villages, but meant that more forest had to be cleared for *their* plantations. The momentary improvement in the road also encouraged further commercial development, resulting in still more clearing of the forest.

This had several results. One rather subtle one was that for the traditional villagers, who lived in fear of the huge forest that surrounded them, that fearful world was now further removed, almost out of sight in comparison with the way it used to dominate both village and plantation. This could not but change the perception of the villagers of themselves in relation to the world around to them. It might also, one would suppose, change their perception of the traditional inhabitants of the forest, the Mbuti hunters. As it turned out, both populations changed more in their relation to the *wazungu* world, white or black, than they did toward each other, since that was clearly the cause of the change. Even the new immigrant villagers, the roadworkers and traders, were often referred to as *wazungu*.

But for the moment, in mid–1970, the political condition was such that the roadside was deserted. There were only the widely dispersed administrative posts, which were also military posts, for even the administrators needed protection. Work on the road had not yet been begun again in any systematic way, so cantonments were far and few between. Where villages had been only the rubble of collapsed mud and wattle walls could be seen through a tangle of undergrowth. What had been lush fields, even the once prosperous commercial plantations, were grown wild. But the forest had been driven back too far for it to take over and reassert itself as it used to, in the old days, in a matter of a few months.

This road runs along barely a degree north of the equator. Formerly cooled both by the proximity of the moist forest hugging its edges and by the shade cast by the giant trees on each side, this highway was now exposed to the equatorial sun and could become mercilessly hot. This may have had the initial effect of drying the surface of a road that formerly had been consistently muddy, making for the easier maintenance of a relatively hard surface. But that surface, baked dry, and the land on either side of it, now created such an updraft of hot air that it diverted the rain clouds overhead and had already begun to affect the climate. What had been at the most lesser and greater rainy seasons became periods of dry and wet, much more truly seasonal. This was most noticeable in the central part of the forest, at Epulu, where seasonal variation had been minimal. Here was yet another factor that would surely affect the relationship between the Mbuti hunters and the village farmers.

As late as 1958, official publications discussing the climate described the Ituri as basically nonseasonal, with an annual rainfall of up to two meters distributed evenly throughout the year, with a slight slackening (referred to locally as either little dry seasons or little rainy seasons) about the months of July and December. This had been my experience throughout my visits back to 1951. More truly seasonal variations, though seldom with any totally dry periods, began instantly, east and west, north and south, wherever the forest gave way to open ground. But in 1970 the second half of the year was virtually dry until October in the central part of the forest, then again in January and February. Only two or three years later Japanese anthropologists found the seasons so firmly established that it did not seem to cross their minds that it had not always been so, just as when I wrote about the Ituri in the sixties it did not cross my mind that in such a vast forest climatic change could come about so speedily.

DeMedina, a great naturalist who spent his whole life in Zaïre, and a good deal of it in the Ituri, was in the Ituri during those crucial years and saw the pattern of the rains change as the central road was steadily converted into a major highway. However, he asserted then (and I found it to be true) that while the roadway was now indeed subject to seasonal change, the rains still fell much as before in the deep forest. The Mbuti also made the same assertion. But the reports by Tadaka, Tanno, and others, and reports coming in now from members of the Harvard team in the eastern part of the forest indicate that not only is the climatic change continuing, but that it may vary quite considerably from one part of the forest to another. This should be more than enough to inhibit any predictions about the future course of sociological change.

For a hundred miles or so on either side of Epulu, although the width of the road was still twice what it had been in colonial times, the forest was not cut back to quite the extent it was further out. But after we left the seat of the government-appointed chief of the Ndaka, at Bafwakoa, there were none of the villages that I had known so well in the past until we arrived at Epulu half a day later. Here and there a single house could be seen under construction, but nothing approaching any sign of village life. This, together with the occasional rusted wreck of an army truck or tank, or an abandoned motor car, gave the impression that the war had wiped out the village population.

At Epulu the roadway leading down to the original village of Camp Putnam had disappeared completely; it was impossible even to see where it had been. The road continued on to where a bridge had replaced the old ford. There to the left was the old *Station de Capture des Okapis*, as the *station de chasse* was later known, and to the right the ruins of what had once been David's proud creation, the *Hotel Domaine des Okapis*. Its walls were crumbling, and its roof had mostly been blown off by bombs or shell fire. A few of the traditional mud and wattle houses roofed with phrynium leaves clung to the side of the road away from the Hotel David, as it had always been known, but these were not the houses of villagers. Rather, they belonged to workers at the okapi-capturing station. The station was just trying to reestablish itself, serving also as an armed administrative post, though officially part of the National Park service. Even so, there was no administrator or Park commandant; the harried clerk who had been left in charge said it was still too dangerous for them.

REFORMATION OF THE VILLAGE WORLD

All the above is described in some detail in the hope that it will evoke at least something of the atmosphere that was such a crucial factor in determining the way in which the village world slowly returned to existence. It was an atmosphere of danger, of fear, of uncertainty. Above all, it was an atmosphere that in itself was totally alien to the forest, suggesting the presence of an alien power, unknown and potentially hostile. It was not the lingering atmosphere of the years of war that had so terribly scarred the forest road. It was something much more alive and vital than that, and every bit as full of danger. It was as though something much more than the physical villages had been destroyed. It was as though the very well-spring of village life had dried up, as though the way of the ancestors that made life itself possible had been destroyed.

Most of the village population that had survived the years of war was still in hiding in the deep forest, with the Mbuti, waiting to see if the war had really ended. During the next few months they emerged, one by one, family by family, but never a village population in its entirety. I established myself under the protection of the National Park, at the friendly but firm request of the clerk. I think he did it as much for his own sense of security as mine. I saw only one face that I had known from before, that of an Mbuti who was told that a *wazungu* by the name of Mulefu had come back. Before a day was over the story had become enlarged, and Mulefu was the son of *Putinam* and was going to give life to the old village of *Campi Putinam*.

Similar things were happening up and down the road. Anything or anyone that could be taken as a symbol of security, *by virtue of their association with the past*, was magnified out of all proportion and became the nucleus of what pretended to be an old village. Just across the river the "old" village of Bandindikpe came to life this way, with old Mandevu emerging from the forest and solemnly building his house right where the old brothel had once been, a symbol of the power of the old ways if ever there was one. And then, just beyond, Vasan emerged and attracted a number of villagers, some of whom were quite new to the area, and recreated the "old" village of Eboyo.

But to the immediate west of Epulu, where the old Ngwana village of Dar es Salaam had been, the site was left untouched, a tangle of secondary vegetation where Musafili had once lived as though the slave traders were still in control of the forest. Musafili was not a bad man at all; I had known him well. But he was a good Muslim and insisted on an open orthodoxy that reminded others a little too vividly of the role his fathers had played in enslaving others. When the Simba came Musafili had fled eastward to the administrative post of Mambasa. Had he stayed where he was known, and where his intolerance of others was taken with good humor and weighed against his generosity and love of palm wine, he would have been safe. But in Mambasa there was nobody to speak for him, and with all the other Ngwana in the village where he had taken refuge he was killed. But everyone said he had only been killed once; that was what they wanted it to be.

Having been classified as Putnam's son I had nothing to do but sit back and watch. Mandevu had emerged on one side of the river, and he was so old he should surely have been dead. On the other, *Putinam* had come back in the body of Mulefu. Both were recognized as forces of the past, and specifically of the traditional past—Mandevu because of his priestly role, now considered more as a prophet, and myself because of Putnam's all-consuming anthropological passion for the traditions and languages of all the village peoples in this region. My own formerly shameful role in being more concerned with the forest world than the village world was ignored, and, as it happened, this time I *had* come to study and work with the sadly neglected villagers. My colleague, a black American, was taken to be a villager himself, and it enhanced my reputation that I should be traveling in such company and not with those Mbuti. The old rivalry evidently had not died, yet the Mbuti seemed to bear no resentment. They merely showed mild astonishment when I said I was going to live in the village, not in the forest, this time.

Within the first few days former villagers began to emerge from the forest, some at Epulu, some from further up or down the road. Although for my purposes I would have preferred them to build a totally new village wherever they wanted, they brought me to where the old trail had led up from the long-unused ford, and looking for markers I could not see at all, slowly began cutting towards the river. They followed almost exactly the old trail, uncovering remains of dwellings on either side, each time exclaiming the name of the person who had lived there. Here again was another change, for as they exclaimed they added, in all too many cases, that such and such a person had died during the years of war. It used to be forbidden to speak the names of the dead in such a manner.

By the time we had cleared a respectable foot trail from the road to the river, where the old Camp Putnam had stood, over half a dozen former villagers had come from the forest, leaving their families behind, to see if it was true that the past was coming to life again. At the river they cleared all the undergrowth, and prodded around until they came upon the old mud floor of Camp Putnam, baked hard before the roof had been put on the house, and further baked by hot fires so that it could still be used to trace the outlines of the new building. Meanwhile the villagers had begun building their own "old" houses, and fetched their wives from the forest to help them. And with the wives came a flurry of Mbuti, anxious to see if the villagers were really leaving the forest at last, and if they were going to build new plantations and grow bananas and manioc and other foods that they could steal.

Up and down the road, sometimes only in twos or threes, villagers emerged. But the return to the past was not always easy. Some villagers were so anxious to break away from the forest world and recreate the old village world that they tried to do this on their own. After those years in the forest they felt they had no further need for the Mbuti, that they had learned enough to be able to supply their own needs. There were plenty of young saplings and fresh phrynium leaves near the road, since no villages had been built for years, so they had no need for Mbuti there. They cut their own small, modest fields, intending to enlarge them as the year went on, but until they bore fruit they were dependent on forest foods. Up and down the road villagers began to die, from injury in the forest, from snakebite, or from eating poisonous roots or mushrooms. In such cases the old village resentment and mistrust of the forest reasserted itself, and with it their attempt to dominate and control the forest people, the Mbuti. But where things went well, as at Epulu and Bandindikpe, the major difference between the new and the old was that the new villages seemed more truly a part of the forest, and in the villages the Mbuti and villagers mingled more freely.

Old beliefs in witchcraft, the unconscious manipulation by certain people of supernatural forces, began to assume more and more importance, explaining, as they had done in the old days, why things went wrong, and, under the guise of "witchcraft accusations," bringing to public attention any wrongdoing anywhere in the village. In this way the return to the way of the ancestors, so earnestly wanted by Buko, began to become a reality. For witchcraft, in this form, and in this area at least, had been a mainstay of that way, drawing attention to any misfortune, however small, as being the consequence of departure from the way, however unintentional. Such a departure in itself looses the forces of the supernatural, which can then work for evil as well as good. Most disputes are settled that way. The blame is attributed to the supernatural rather than to individuals, though individuals (usually a great many of them) may be held responsible for digressing too far from the way.

But as yet there were no charges of sorcery, which occurs when that same supernatural force is deliberately, consciously manipulated by an individual for his or her own individual good, and thus for the harm of others. In this system, priests are close indeed to sorcerers. Both work in precisely the same way. Both use the same techniques for manipulating the supernatural, but whereas the priest manipulates it for the good of society, the sorcerer works only for the harm of society. The last accusation of sorcery that I had heard was against "Bwana David." Perhaps that was why Mandevu built his house where he did, where he could look across to that old site of evil. It was certainly why nobody built anywhere near the hotel ruins for the longest time, and why none of the old villagers would go anywhere near it. I was not allowed to go by myself, and only grudgingly was allowed to go when some Mbuti offered to take me, for their power over the supernatural was more than enough to protect against that of a dead sorcerer.

The Mbuti laughed as they showed me where the Simba had stood, just as Buko told me, and scared the villagers and *wazungu* alike simply because they were dressed like Mbuti in bark cloth and carried bows and arrows. They were more modest in their account of Simba immortality, and they showed me a sinister circular mound to one side of the hotel, about forty feet across, where they said that many bodies were buried, both Simba and *wazungu*. When I asked who had buried them they said that Mbuti had done it, "because villagers and *wazungu* smell so terrible" it would have killed the forest to have left them in the open.

It was significant that when sorcery became a factor in the post-independence village world, the very first accusations were against black *wazungu*, who had moved into the old hotel grounds and were beginning to live in the ruins. And it was near that burial ground, if that is what it was, that evil spirits were first to be seen, carrying blue plastic buckets, looking for female throats to cut. But for the time, as the villages were reforming, such drastic innovations were still unneeded. The process of adaptation still had enough strength to draw on, and for a time it seemed as though Buko's dream would come true.

Up and down the road villagers emerged from the forest and began to cluster together and form villages, nearly always taking the name of the village that used to occupy that territory. Sometimes the name indicated a founding individual, sometimes a lineage or clan. The same tendencies were at work now, new villages being formed either around powerful (charismatic) individuals, such as Mandevu, without regard for lineage, or by members of a single lineage coming together. Some villages grew into tight-knit corporate lineal units, while others grew in size and complexity, eventually comprising members not only of different clans, but even of different tribes.

In fact, it was rare for one of these new villages not to have at least one stranger incorporated into its fold, and usually the stranger was adopted into one of the local lineages. Even the strongly traditional village of Kopu, which, under the leadership of its founder, Kopu himself, had been one of the major centers of Bira ritual activity, adopted a Mangbetu from the far north of the forest into the senior lineage. He had fled into the forest during the years of war and had somehow crossed into the southern sector. There he joined the small group of villagers led by Yuma, Kopu's lineal successor, which had attached itself to one of the Mbuti groups living furthest into the deep forest. And when the Mangbetu fell sick he was taken into Yuma's own household and cared for there as a member of the immediate family. When he died he was buried as a full member of the lineage, with almost as much pomp as I had seen Kopu himself buried, so many years earlier. It is not that strangers were sought so much as that they were readily welcomed and given almost preferential treatment.

Mandevu insisted that the village that grew up around him remain small, and all its male members were important ritual figures. As small as the village was (five houses), it included members of the Lese, Bira, Ndaka, and Budo peoples. And Mandevu himself lived in isolation, tended only by Katchelewa, his son by an Mbuti wife, destined to become a powerful ritual figure in his own right. So the Mbuti also were represented in that one tiny village of Bandindikpe, one of the most powerful villages in the forest.

POLITICAL REALIGNMENTS

This represented a development or adaptation of the historical tendency for villages at the extremities of tribal territory to form strong and effective, as well as affective, intertribal links. A new development, it seemed, was that these same medial villages now more consciously integrated some Mbuti into their midst. This was accomplished, if possible, through intermarriage, but if not, then by according them privileged status and allowing them unusual roles in traditional village rituals from which they had previously been excluded.

In the center of tribal territories the relationship between villagers and Mbuti went back pretty much to what it used to be, one of relatively good-natured mutual exploitation—the villagers deriving economic benefit from the relationship (forest products and a small amount of labor), while the Mbuti had their essentially political need satisfied, namely the exclusion of the villagers from their hunting territories. Once again, villagers began to lay claim to their hereditary role as kpara (patrons) of specific Mbuti lineages. This was a prime source of intervillage dispute, since each village had members whose claims as kpara were formerly appropriate in another territory, and since most members of the new village had created new *kpara* relationships with whichever Mbuti band had protected them during the years of war. These new relationships as often as not ran quite counter to the earlier "lineal" claims. Thus villagers started initiating disputes against each other for having "stolen" each other's Mbuti clients. And, as always, this made not the slightest difference to the Mbuti, since their band composition continued to change every month, as it had always done, so that any permanent lineal relationship was in reality an effective impossibility, however convenient as a model for the villagers.

In the centrally located villages, then, the Mbuti were less incorporated into village life and continued to be excluded from any participation in village ritual life, except in the subordinate roles sometimes demanded by the ritual itself. In the medial villages, however, the concept of hereditary *kpara*, which even there had formerly been maintained as a myth (Putnam was compelled to make restitution, as was any adopted stranger in those days, to *kpara* whose Mbuti clients shifted their nominal allegiance to him) was now almost completely dropped. As Putnam's heir, for instance, I inherited his former wife, Mada, and others claiming to be his children, as my mother and siblings. But I was told that the Mbuti who had regarded him as their *kpara* were now considered as part of the village as a whole, without any special individual patron/client trading relationships. And so it was, also, across the river at Bandindikpe, and at other medial villages.

THE UNIFYING FORCE OF TRADITION

No sooner had these new villages begun to take shape and clear the bush around them for new fields of manioc and banana plantations than talk began of holding the first *nkumbi* since the beginning of the years of war. According to Dr. Joseph Towles, who studied the ritual in minute detail, the *nkumbi,* customarily held once every three years, is the very heart of traditional life. Through the beliefs it expresses in its incredibly rich language of natural symbols, music, song, and dance, it nourishes and keeps flowing the life blood of the social order. As he also points out, the *nkumbi* is an institution that has spread into the forest from the east, and has been adopted by nearly all the peoples in the forest, serving the important political function of providing them all, regardless of their disparate tribal origins and mutually incomprehensible languages, with a common sense of spiritual identity. It is through the *nkumbi* that the villagers and Mbuti are able to present a united political front and share a common sentiment, holding to a common good, while still retaining that vital sense of distinction. The *nkumbi* serves as an example in action of the principle of opposition without hostility.

In the new context of independence that same principle was at work. The years of war had forced disparate peoples together in the face of a common enemy (white and black *wazungu*). But with the talk of an approaching *nkumbi*, whatever hostility might have remained, attaching itself to the black *wazungu* at the Epulu national park station or to myself, evaporated. On the contrary, every effort was made to incorporate us into the *nkumbi*. This seemed also be the experience of Dr. Towles as he attended one *nkumbi* after another while it spread, in tradi-

It is ironical that the nkumbi, *held by missionaries and administrators to be opposed to all progress, was responsible for the remarkably rapid reestablishment of a flourishing village world following the years of war.*

tional fashion, from village to village, traveling eastward. There was increased emphasis on the rules that compelled a number of adjacent villages to combine their efforts instead of each holding its own initiation. There was comment on the *nkumbi* being that much more strong when even different tribes were incorporated, each of the houseposts of the initiation hut being put in place by men of different origins. Everything combined to reduce any latent hostility, if not to eradicate it, while making no attempt to disguise the opposition.

And in many instances this, the most traditional of all rituals in the Ituri, adapted its custom of appointing a senior villager as "the father of the *nkumbi*." They adapted it to the new political context, which, in this remote part of Zaïre, they barely understood, by clothing the "father" so that he quite unmistakably resembled the popular picture of President Mobutu Seseko, complete with leopardskin hat and dark glasses. That visual image was about all that was known of the new nation by the villagers, yet they sensed a new political reality and actively sought through their tradition to incorporate the new nation into their midst. This was even before the first general elections were held in this area. The people themselves took the first step towards recognition of yet another opposition without hostility.

For months the sacred *makata* sticks and initiation drums resounded along the road. Initiations started as soon as the first crops from the new plantations were ready. But the initiation had not been held for so long that age-structured roles were all out of kilter. Those old enough to be priests were the only ones practiced in the art of circumcision; they had had no opportunity to teach a younger generation. The youths and young men who should have occupied that role, by virtue of their age, were themselves still uncircumcised. And those slightly older had not learned the craft; the only circumcision they had witnessed was their own.

In one place at least, there was a formal dispute between a former ritual circumciser, who argued that he should be allowed to circumcise on this occasion, to teach the younger men, and the traditionalists, who insisted that purity was more important than technical expertise, and that the *nkumbi* would only be effective if done with absolute dedication to purity. That this meant that the circumcisions would be performed by young men who had never done it before was immaterial, they said. It would be inviting much greater disaster to prefer technical expertise to ritual purity. The ritual doctor, Kekeke, insisted. The traditionalists put a curse on him, and in front of my eyes I saw a good old friend since we were both little more than youths ourselves begin to die. And die he did. It was his only way of reconciling his beliefs, tainted as they were with a western concept of hygiene and technical skill, and his deep respect for the tradition in which he should have been a priest. The circumcision was performed in many cases by youngsters who had indeed never seen any except their own. But the traditionalists were right; there was nothing but success and joy throughout the forest.

Mbuti, as formerly, held a relatively subordinate role, but this time there was much greater emphasis on the *ritual* necessity for their presence. They also took a much more prominent part than ever before in the various *baraza* discussions concerning the running of the *nkumbi*. Seated among the villagers in the *baraza* they discussed as equals. And into those same *baraza*, though not during the *nkumbi*, they sometimes brought their sacred *molimo* trumpet from the forest, to help the villagers "rejoice" the village, just as the Mbuti always use the *molimo*, in their forest world, to "rejoice" the forest.

BLACK *WAZUNGU*: THE NEW OUTSIDERS

Adaptation was working everywhere, it seemed, not simply to restore an old tradition, however valuable and vital, but to use old traditions, customs, and beliefs

Mandevu, the greatest ritual figure in the southern Ituri, stood for all that was good in the past and encouraged all that was good in the present. In dress and thought he was the very antithesis of the black wazungu, *but, while rejecting their values, he never said a word against them.*

to accommodate to the new context of independence. There was enough political sophistication, even in this isolated and nonliterate region, to recognize that the central authority of the colonials had been replaced by another, equally undesirable, central authority of black *wazungu*, linked to the name of Tshombe, and that this was what their friends, the Simba, the followers of Patriko (Lumumba), had resisted in the years of war.

As far as the villagers were concerned the Simba had won. They had not been defeated, they merely disappeared, as was within their power, having achieved their goal. Indeed, it was not long after my arrival that some extremely influential villagers who had been held in prison in Bunia under suspicion of being Simba leaders were released. One had been a powerful chief that I had known long ago, and whose politics were always suspect even in those days. He was under sentence of death, and his unexpected release and return to the seat of the government-appointed chief at the village of Koki was taken as yet another sign that the Simba had won, and that whoever was in control now, the person with the leopard skin hat and dark glasses, must indeed be on the right side.

Adaptation had worked a political miracle. But unfortunately this was not recognized by the local administrators, nearly all of them completely foreign to this area, many from a thousand miles away, who took the customary manifestations of opposition to indicate hostility. Expecting hostility (and really they can hardly be blamed) they thought they saw it all around them: in the enthusiastic manifestations of tribal identity and even more in the massive show of intertribal unity displayed by the *nkumbi*, which now was even drawing some of the noncircumcisers in the northeast Ituri into their confederation. The administration established more and more appointed chiefs and subchiefs, and posted other officials in almost every major village throughout the area. The head of the Parks station at Epulu came to take control, and with him came a virtual small army, a contingent that paraded in military fashion every morning. It was not intended as an offensive move, but rather "to show the flag." However, since the misunderstanding was mutual, the villagers took this as an offensive and hostile move. They began to regard the new administration, instead of being part of their tradition, worthy of incorporation into the *nkumbi* confederation, as being hostile and dangerous outsiders, more black *wazungu*.

DeMedina, one of the greatest of the colonial naturalists, himself half African, and well respected as having always respected the rightness of tradition, was in residence at Epulu just before the new head came to take over. He invited me for an evening meal one evening, and had the cook serve me. His own food he cooked himself on a little charcoal stove. He told me not to worry, it was only him "they" were trying to poison. I asked who "they" were, and he laughed and said "the black *wazungu*, which was what they always used to call me!" Two days later he was dead, of poison. And his skin, those who saw his body said, had turned blue.

A youth fell into the river while fishing from rocks near the bridge. He was seen to wave and disappear below the surface. A crowd gathered to wait for him to reappear, although the water flows so fast through those rapids that anything floating is quickly swept downstream. By the time I arrived there was a large crowd standing there, silently, still looking at the spot where the youth had slipped beneath the water. I asked if there would be any harm in my trying to find him, since they were sure he was still there. They said no, but it was no good, as it was a work of sorcery. Nonetheless I tried, and a Zande youth followed me. Together we dove below the swirling surface, and had to fight to avoid being swept down under the bridge. But the crowd continued to let us look down there. Suddenly the Zande came up to the surface and shouted that he had found the body. He immediately swam ashore and disappeared into the bush.

The body had, in fact, snagged on submerged rocks. I brought it ashore and we tried artificial respiration, but of course it was useless, though we worked for nearly half an hour. All the time the crowd stood by and watched without any comment, except to say that what I was doing was useless, since this was sorcery. There was evil about. When I stood back there was a gasp, for the youth looked as though he had suffered nothing. His body and hair were in perfect order, and his knife was still tucked neatly in his belt. Then it was discovered that he was uncircumcised. Perhaps he was the source of evil; he was certainly a stranger. And it was a Zande (noncircumcisers from the north) who had joined me and who had known where to find the body.

The body was carried to Bandindikpe, *makata* sticks were hastily cut and the circumcision drums brought out, and with full ritual the boy was prepared for circumcision. The next day the ritual was completed and the body was buried. The *nkumbi* had been invoked to combat the evil that had come into the forest.

First there was Kekeke, then DeMedina, now this strange youth. Then there was the death of the Mangbetu boy at Kopu's village. It was remembered that Bira and Ndaka chiefs had fought each other recently at Epulu (actually the Bira chief had got extremely drunk while celebrating the New Year and did not know what he was doing or who he was fighting). And Hamadi, the Bira who had been condemned to death as a Simba leader and then released, had on the same occasion accused Ndaka villagers of not feeding him properly and had uttered a curse. And total foreigners (Nande entrepreneurs from the far southeast of the forest and the head of the station) had established restaurants and hotels on the road at Epulu. Nobody knew what went on there, for villagers were always excluded. (Actually, that was not quite true, certainly not of the Nande restaurant.) Plainly the source of this new evil was at Epulu. Epulu by then had become the most important government post in the central region of the forest, second in importance only to the administrative capital, Mambasa. It was also noted that the mission, from the far side of Mambasa, had established a little roadside church where the old market used to be, and that there had been fighting when the villagers continued to hold their market on Sundays when a service was going on.

THE SUBVERSION OF TRADITION

So I was not unduly surprised when one day, while I was sitting in the Nande restaurant with my colleague, a uniformed member of the station (they all wore army uniforms except the local villagers) came rushing in and said that two "invisible" blue spirits, *saitani*, had been seen down near the river, behind the old Hotel David, and attacked his wife and another woman. They were carrying blue plastic buckets and had wanted to fill them with blood to drink. The story caused some interest, but most of us were more interested in the fact that this man seemed so genuinely scared. Surely he did not believe such an idiotic story, just the kind of story you would expect the local villagers to tell, not *Zaïroises*, not *citoyens*. This was just before midday.

By early afternoon more reports were coming in, and women were named from other villages down the road (the direction from which the *nkumbi* always comes, was the thought that crossed my mind). These women had been caught by invisible blue spirits; their throats had been cut and the *saitani* had held them up above the blue plastic buckets and drained all the blood from them and made off with the blood to drink it. Then the bodies became invisible too.

Other reports came that these people were indeed missing, and this was confirmed the next day. At noon the next day Epulu was as if in a state of siege. The head of the station, normally very elegant and military, came rushing into the Nande restaurant and ordered all his men back to the station. He looked as though he had seen the *saitani* himself. He said he was ordering all his men to put away their guns and take up bows and arrows. Guns were useless against these *saitani*, just as they were useless against the Simba. That last remark marked the end of the remarkable process of voluntary, even eager adaptation to the new political context on the part of local tradition. It established not just an opposition, but a confrontation filled with hostility, for it aligned the station, hence the central government, clearly against the Simba, the world of the new nation against the village world.

The military commandant, in full uniform but himself clutching a bow and arrow, then asked me to intercede with the Mbuti, since I knew them so well. He wanted me to ask them to come in from the forest and protect the village, since no *saitani* would attack their own people. While it would be difficult to document, I think that it was from this moment that the newly blossoming relationship between villagers and Mbuti, another adaptive development, began to wither. The villagers, remembering the problems they encountered when first coming out of the forest, trying to get food for themselves and so many dying up and down the road from poisoned food (for that is how they now began to see it—it was no longer merely due to poisonous food) began to say that those things that they had thought to be witchcraft were perhaps in reality sorcery. Perhaps they had been wrong to let the Mbuti come so close. Perhaps they had been wrong to welcome foreigners, even Lese, Zande, Mangbetu, and Budo, into their village. They began to invoke the old *kpara* relationships and demand that "their" Mbuti come in and protect them. (The air of hysteria was so pervasive that my colleague and I both decided to have Mbuti patrol our own house, with bows and arrows, for the next few nights.) In a matter of just a few days the lines were drawn, perhaps not irrevocably, but clearly enough to undo the work of adaptation and make future adaptation unlikely, if not impossible.

The alignment of the village world against the world of national government was finally completed when one day a sleek Mercedes drove into Epulu from Kisangani, with two investigators from the central government to find out what was happening: Why were so many people being killed, and how was this revolutionary movement to be put down? The investigators stepped out of the Mercedes, wearing splendid dark pin-striped suits, and both of them were nervously holding onto little bows and arrows, thoughtfully provided by some Mbuti further down the road. As far as the villagers were concerned this clearly stated the government's position: The government was siding with the Mbuti, and by their own accusations were hostile to the villagers, holding them responsible for all the killings. This opinion was confirmed by the government's announcement of a program for the *"emancipation des pygmées,"* and by the almost simultaneous introduction of a program for the taxation of villagers. Here was evil indeed, and here was an end to any thought of adaptation.

Mention has to be made here of the unwitting role played by the missions at this juncture, for it was just at this moment that they were reestablishing themselves. For them any talk of evil, of witchcraft and sorcery, let alone talk of invisible spirits carrying blue plastic buckets to be filled with human blood, was all evidence that they were still faced with the original heart of darkness, with bestial savagery. They were not prepared to take the anthropological approach, to see that these beliefs were merely the way in which another culture expressed its political and economic problems and sought to deal with them while arousing an absolute minimum of animosity. The missionaries were much more eager to believe that killings were actually taking place, and the drinking of human blood, and even that some kind of malevolent spiritual force had been invoked, than they were to admit to the reality that nothing of the sort had ever taken place. Even as the women whose blood had allegedly been drunk reappeared from wherever they had gone for a visit, the story persisted in mission circles that some killings, and other unspeakable acts, had actually taken place. It confirmed their felt need to convert, and they extended their efforts.

By the non-Christian Africans this was perceived as an actively hostile move, aimed directly at subverting the rule of tradition. The fact that the government spoke in the name of Christianity and allied itself with the efforts of the missions did neither institution any good in the eyes of the villagers. It merely increased the sense of danger and widened the gap the *nkumbi* had so remarkably narrowed.

While not all missions were as ignorant and as openly hostile as were a few, the few effectively destroyed the credibility of the others. In one, for instance, a newly arrived nurse offered to give her class of African students an afternoon in the mission swimming pool, since the fee was too high for any of them to enjoy such a thing on their own. One afternoon, when the missionaries were taking their siesta, the nurse made her Christmas gift, and her class plunged into the pool. Within twenty minutes it was being emptied by order of one of the head medical missionaries, and it was scrubbed before it was refilled. Arriving at another mission with my black American colleague, I was invited into a meal, and told that my African servant could get something to eat in the native quarters. An interracial married couple, on the American consulate staff, were denied joint accommodation at another (American) mission.

Such incidents alone, though not characteristic of all missions by any means, were sufficient to do the damage. Other stories began to circulate, such as the story that it was the missionaries who liked to drink human blood. After all, it was in their scriptures; they said so in their ritual, the same ritual in which they ate human flesh. And, in their mission hospitals had they not been seen, every day, taking blood from victims? And what were all those blue plastic buckets doing in mission hospitals?

The overt hostility of the missions to all things traditional, combined with their close association with the central government, by whose permission they were allowed to exist, made the government look guilty by association. By the end of one year the situation was almost back to where it had been prior to independence, as far as the village world was concerned. The villages had taken the essential initial step toward incorporation, and had been rejected. All government measures, as they appeared to the villagers, were designed, as were those of the colonials, to feather the government's nest at the expense of the villagers. The villagers were treated as inferior beings by government officials, just as they had been by the colonials. Why else should attempts be made to make them dress and speak like *wazungu* instead of what they were? The village world retreated into itself, as before, playing the government's game for what they could get out of it and no more.

And just as it saw itself being assailed from the outside by the government, so it saw itself also being assailed from within, by the Mbuti, who for some reason were strongly supported by the government. The adaptation that had begun to bring the two populations closer together suddenly gave way to an open hostility that had never existed before. The very term *citoyen*, which the villagers had proudly adopted, even incorporating it into the *nkumbi*, now became a term of abuse. For the government had made a public pronouncement that from now on the *"pygmées"* were to have full and equal rights; they were to be "emancipated" from bondage, for they were *"citoyens"* like everyone else. Of course they were not like everyone else at all, and since the proclamation amused the Mbuti, who knew they had never been in bondage to start with, they made a point of always addressing each other as *citoyen* when they were in the village world. The villagers, who had begun to see "citizenship" as being something akin to being a member of the *nkumbi* confederation, promptly rejected the term, and stopped using it except as a term of contempt to be reserved for Mbuti and black *wazungu*.

Ironically, at about this time, knowing nothing of the political convulsions taking place in this isolated part of his country, President Mobutu issued another proclamation, saying that wherever it still existed the traditional form of initiation of youth into manhood should be preserved, and elsewhere it should be reintroduced. For whereas youths could learn the skills necessary for adult life in the new schools being built everywhere, it was in traditional rites such as the *nkumbi* that they learned to be real people: citizens.

6/The forest world

NORMALIZATION AND ADAPTATION

During all of this the Mbuti were by no means unaffected, and by no means were they passive onlookers. They did not stay back in the deep forest, where they had been for the duration of the years of war, though they could have. Once the villages were reestablished the Mbuti were more evident along the roadside than they ever were during the colonial era. Several factors encouraged this, such as the change to a more truly seasonal climate in which the needs of villagers for help in their fields was, though reduced, correspondingly seasonal. As the roadside population was swelled by the establishment of cantonments and administrative posts, traders and shopkeepers, the demand for forest products, as well as for forest labor, was virtually doubled. It was surprising to me that in all the villages I visited, regardless of whether the Mbuti tended to be incorporated, as with medial villages, or kept at a ritual distance, the villagers quickly readopted their former apparent fear of the forest. Despite the protection it had afforded them, they refused to venture far into it even when in need.

The Mbuti insisted that despite the extraordinary change of climate along the road, and the lack of rainfall between July and October of that first year, the rainfall in the deep forest was as plentiful as ever, and so was the amount of game. They also claimed that throughout the years of war they had not (in that central region at least) suffered any hunger, although they missed the luxury of village foods. They had taken to eating more forest vegetables that they had given up when they had easy access to village products. They referred to these as "war foods." They never brought me any to see or taste, though they promised often enough: After all, I had chosen the role of villager for this field trip, so they were going to treat me as one. For one whole year I did not set foot inside the deep forest, visiting only those camps within an easy morning's reach of the village, though even some of those were a little far for the taste of most villagers.

I confined myself on this trip primarily to the Ndaka and Bira tribal territories, stretching along the road from NiaNia to Mambasa, with Epulu being slightly beyond the midpoint. Dr. Towles worked on the far (south) side of the Ituri, where there was no road, in the much more inaccessible territory of the Mbo. There are no significant differences between his data for that part of the forest and my own.

I was also somewhat surprised at the rapidity with which Mbuti established camps on the outskirts of most villages. In the colonial era nearly all villages had such attached encampments, occupied sporadically by whatever Mbuti came to trade with that village. But these had grown up gradually over the years. When a new village was built it was sometimes as long as a year before such an Mbuti village-camp took shape. Not only that, but these new village-camps nearly always had at least a few Mbuti living there, though the same people never stayed for much longer than a week, it seemed. One other difference was that whereas the old village-camps had mostly been built (very badly) of mud and wattle, in imitation of the village style of housebuilding, these village-camps were built in the traditional Mbuti manner: hemispherical frames of saplings hung with phrynium leaves.

At first I was not sure whether it was because I was now "being a villager," or whether it indicated some change in the overall Mbuti/villager relationship, but the Mbuti kept addressing me by the name the villagers had always called me by, *Mulefu*. They brushed aside the fact that they had always called me by another name in their own language (a Bira dialect), *Ebamunyama*. I also noticed that whereas many of the women and a few of the older men had before seemed not to be able to speak KiNgwana, the *lingua franca* of the whole province, now everyone spoke it fluently. Mulefu is a KiNgwana name. I was told that a lot of the young Mbuti, boys and girls that were just children, or not even born, when I left just before independence, hardly knew their own language. It made sense in that the clusters of villagers attached to Mbuti bands during the years of war were not always homogeneous, so *they* must have often been compelled to use KiNgwana, both among each other and with the Mbuti.

But something more than this seemed to be at work. The villagers too were often preferring to speak KiNgwana rather than their old languages. Only when the old men got together to discuss a local dispute involving their own lineage could you be reasonably sure of not hearing any KiNgwana. Yet KiNgwana was the language of the very people who the villagers had frequently pointed out to the Simba as deserving of death, and the language was basically that of the Arab slave traders, being a form of Swahili. A Bira youth, in his late teens, knew almost as little conversational KiBira as I did, and I knew more of their ritual language than he did. It proved to be much the same with the Mbuti.

At first I attributed it to the fact that I was being a villager and living in the village. I remembered how the Mbuti had refused to sing their own songs for me on my very first visit, nearly thirty years previously, unless I came with them into the forest. So when I failed in my efforts to check up on earlier field data concerning their forest beliefs and forest life, I started visiting hunting camps close enough for a few daring villagers to visit. But even there the young people expressed ignorance of such key terms as *ekimi* and *akami*. Significantly though, they allowed *some* superficial knowledge of what *ekimi* was, while denying flatly any knowledge of the more negative value of *akami*. Elders simply brushed my questions aside or diverted the conversation into other channels.

Then I saw the *molimo* brought into a village *baraza* one night, just as secretively as it is sometimes brought into a forest camp—suddenly there, and just as suddenly, after singing awhile, not there. When this was repeated on several other occasions of minor crisis in the village I knew that the change in language usage and the apparent ignorance of old ritual terms among the Mbuti was not due to that old barrier that had separated the two worlds, most of all their rituals, so completely.

Similarly, I found Mbuti in the village-camps who seemed to restrict kinship terms to their biological kin instead of extending them to their classificatory kin (virtually anyone living in the same camp at the same time). At first I attributed this to relatively normal behavior, for them, in the village context. But then I saw that although the old hereditary Mbuti-*kpara* relationship had to a large extent broken down, individual Mbuti families attached themselves to specific villagers in other ways. While they shared their services and goods with all, individual Mbuti families seemed to develop a strong affective relationship with individual villager families that were not their *kpara*. They could often be seen passing the time of day at the door to the village household, or in that family's *baraza*. They sometimes referred to such a household collectively as *karé*, a village term that had been restricted to "those who saw the knife" together, that is, fellow *nkumbi* initiates.

REDUCTION OF RITUAL DISTANCE

This was all part of the greater proximity that the years of war had brought about, bringing the two populations closer to each other in more than a physical sense, and for more reasons than mere economic or political need.

When the *nkumbi* season was opened the Mbuti found themselves in popular demand. They were wanted not just to do some of the physical work involved, nor just to bring in supplies of forest meat to feast the guests during the preliminary festivities, nor even for the forest materials essential for the construction of the camp and initiation house itself. The concern for their presence expressed among the villagers in their *baraza* discussions was that "we are one people now, we need them to lend their strength to the boys." They were referring to what they regarded as the supernatural strength of the Mbuti, the power of the forest. In the colonial era the reason given for Mbuti participation had always centered on the boys themselves, and on the economic relationships brought about by cutting the boys in pairs, always linking one village boy with one Mbuti boy in the special bond brotherhood of *karé*. It also asserted the superiority of the villagers, as they saw it, by cutting the Mbuti boy first, "to clean the knife." Now the focus was on adult participation. And the need to circumcise the boys was seen as an opportunity to achieve a quite different kind of alliance, an alliance between the supernatural of both worlds.

It was still on village terms, but now for the first time the Mbuti could make some demands of their own, and had a very real power of their own. And at Epulu, Katchelewa Bangama, the son of Mandevu by his Mbuti wife, reared by other Mbuti in the forest, and always considered by villagers as an Mbuti, emerged as one of the chief circumcisers. In fact, he was the only one for whom the ill-fated Kekeke had a good word to say, even though Katchelewa had never yet performed the operation or been trained in the work.

As if to make it plain what an important departure this was from the old rule that Mbuti must have no part in the actual ritual and hold no ritual office, Katchelewa donned the dress of the Bira ritual doctors, and announced that since this was the first *nkumbi* for so long, and there was so much weakness in all the villages, he was going to give strength to the village by performing the circumcision with his teeth. Even Kekeke, who had some pretty odd ways of his own, denounced that, though he made the mistake of doing so in the name of western hygiene. Other ritual specialists denounced it because, properly performed, the circumcision should be done with the old ritual knives only. Kekeke was in favor of straight-edge razors. But Katchelewa was undaunted, and because he had the double power of both the forest and the village, and because Mandevu smiled every time Katchelewa spoke, nobody other than Kekeke denied Katchelewa the right to perform the circumcision as he thought best. Astutely, Mandevu's Mbuti son compromised, and circumcised by holding the ritual knife between his teeth. And he circumcised only the Mbuti boys on that occasion.

All this made me wonder if the Mbuti were not in the process of assimilation. They seemed always ready to bring in from the forest whatever the villagers needed, and to help them with work in their fields. But cotton growing had long been abandoned, and the roadside population had not yet begun to make unduly heavy demands on forest produce. And even though there seemed to be many more Mbuti on the roadside, at any one time, than there had ever been before, there were obviously many still in the forest, since there was no real shortage of forest products, including game. Rather than assimilating, the Mbuti too were adapting to a new context, developing the new proximity discovered during the years of war.

But then the central government, determined to make this unproductive part of the nation contribute to the national economy, began to develop the Epulu station. It became a major government center, technically under the department of National Parks. It had been a small station of one or two acres, where captured okapi were reared and elephants were trained for heavy work. It expanded into an army post that was also geared to send out hunting and trapping parties for the purpose of capturing a wide variety of forest fauna for sale to foreign zoos.

The Africans imported for this work had none of the local village fear of the forest. Up and down the road they cleared trails leading to traps set for okapi and other animals. They first banned all hunting, even by Mbuti, then tried to settle for a modified seasonal ban, at least within the ever-expanding boundaries of this new national park. The park itself, and Epulu village, promised to become a major tourist attraction, and plans were laid for rebuilding the old Hotel David, now occupied by immigrant squatters. The village of Epulu, from being a few houses accommodating the few station workers, grew into what was almost a small township, completely bypassing the trail leading down to the traditional village. The Mbuti village-camp disintegrated for a while, then reformed close to the traditional village in more permanent form.

It was about then that Teleabo Kengé suggested to me that it was time to go back to the forest, to see, once again, the river Lelo, "the most beautiful place in the forest," where there was always *ekimi*. It was time to get away from this world of *akami*. And by then, I confess, my old prejudices were reasserting themselves. I was beginning to regret that I had made the academically justifiable decision to spend this field trip looking at the village world rather than that of the forest. The *akami* was too evident, and growing all the time. So, very early one morning, Kengé having told his wife to stay behind, and having equally arbitrarily ordered half a dozen youths to accompany us and carry our few belongings, I returned to the forest world.

CONTEXTUAL KINSHIP

If I ever had any doubts about the accuracy of my earlier reports on the beauty of the forest, and on the almost complete contrast it presents with the village, they were dispelled within a matter of minutes. Not more than a few hundred yards from the edge of a village plantation it was as though the village world had never existed. The sky was shut out by a mass of foliage high overhead; the sounds of the village were quickly lost. The crowing of roosters was the last sound I heard until all were replaced by the myriad forest sounds—rustles, rumbles, whispers, tap-tap-tappings, snappings, and thumpings, providing a muffled foundation for the buildup of the sounds of all the living things that burrow and crawl and run and jump and fly in this living forest world of the Mbuti. Whatever else had changed, there was no change that I could detect here.

Nor was there any change in the reaction of the young Mbuti who were with us, themselves making forest sounds and shouting out to the forest, "*Ema, Eba, zu kidi, zu kidi 'o!'* "— "Mother, Father, We are coming!" But I noticed that they had changed from KiNgwana into their own language, that distinctively musical form of KiBira. Before I would not even have noticed it, so *there* was change number one. I also noticed that Kengé was much less boisterous than he usually was, in village or forest.

It was not long before I began to notice other things, the most important of which was barely discernible, and at first I made no mention of it. I noticed leaves, some dry and some green, lying oddly on the trail. It was something about their position that was odd; they did not seem quite a part of the whole mass of leaves on which they rested. It was as though they had just blown there, except that there was no wind. And all these leaves looked as though they had once been curled up and burrowed through by an insect, or had their ends nibbled at. They occurred at irregular intervals, sometimes singly, sometimes in small clusters. Finally it seemed that wherever there was a fork in the trail, or a place where it looked as though a tiny antelope trail crossed the narrow foot trail, there would be one or more of those leaves, a few yards before or beyond the crossing. I picked some of them up, and saw Kengé look at me, but he said nothing. Finally I had quite a collection, and discerned a distinct pattern. Some had a bite taken out of the end. Others had been bored through vertically. Some had been pierced horizontally. A few merely had a single hole right through the middle.

By now Kengé, in that familiar old mocking, aggressive way of his, was obviously bursting with impatience for me to say something stupid. So I asked him what kind of insects had made these different patterns. When he asked me why I wanted to know I said that I had never noticed them before, during all the years I had spent in the forest. "That's because they weren't there," he said. It was my turn to ask "why?" and his answer was a curt "We didn't need them." Then he gave a snort and doubled up with laughter. He called a halt, and we all sat down. Stretching out his leg he carefully took a twig and on his thigh, the pressure of the twig leaving a clean gray mark as though his skin were a slate, he drew the familiar kinship signs he had learned from me many years back. "That's what those leaves are," he said, "but we only need them in times of war. That's why you never saw them."

It was a slight blow to my pride, as I had made much of the lack of attention paid by the Mbuti to lineage. Further checking revealed that these were indeed clan symbols: The leaf with the bite out of the end was the baboon clan; the one with spots running horizontally was the leopard clan, and so forth. But they named totemic affiliations rather than clan names, for many of the clan names I had recorded were simply the names of villages at the periphery of some hunting territory. I had seldom heard clan names used in the forest context, even in discussing prospective marriages, or in discussions relating to death. This seemed a natural correlative of the fact that in the Mbuti social system there are neither wealth nor power nor position to inherit. The only times that clan names were mentioned were in relationship to the village context, and certainly the villagers used them as a device by which they could trace the affiliation of specific Mbuti to specific *kpara*.

So almost the moment I thought I had come across a hidden Mbuti kinship system (which would of course have greatly enhanced my reputation as an anthropologist) I was given information that showed that even this limited use of clan totems was related to a foreign context, that of war. Further cross checking revealed that while these totemic symbols were left on the trails by Mbuti, they were primarily a device for identifying both themselves and which kind of villagers were traveling with them.

The nature of Mbuti verbal information about anything that does not occur in the immediate present, at the very moment of speaking preferably, is such that I am still unsure as to the true significance of these leaf symbols. The fact that they were all linked to natural symbols rather than clan/village names suggests that they had more to do with Mbuti needs than village needs, and were an Mbuti system of classification. Without actually seeing them in use and being able to document the circumstances, I would not even want to hazard a guess as to their function. What the Mbuti said has its own significance, and it was very definitely yet another change that had taken place in the forest.

FOREST VALUES REASSERTED

We reached the Lelo river in the afternoon. About a hundred yards before it crossed our trail, Kengé told the youths to stay where they were, that he and I were going on alone. I remembered what he had said about going back to the Lelo, to sing once again, to find *ekimi*. This was the other side of that same complex character I had known for so many years. He could at one moment be the greatest extrovert, and the next moment he would be shut up tight within himself. He could be more of a villager than the villagers, but all Mbuti agreed that, unpredictable as he was, he was all Mbuti, and knew more of the forest than just about anyone other than the *mangésé*. And he even knew more than some of them, many added.

When we got to the banks of the river it was, for me, an emotional moment, because this was indeed where we had spent so many happy days, weeks, months, so many years ago, before the days of war. This was where the Mbuti in that territory said you could always find *ekimi*; for them it was the most beautiful place in the forest. Any hunting camp near the Lelo was bound to be a good camp. For me it brought back happy, good, rich memories of the past. For Kengé it may have done that, but not quite that. Mbuti think differently and see differently. While I just stood and looked at this lovely river, still splashed with the same sunlight, it seemed, as it had always been, Kengé stooped over, cupped some water in his hand and let it trickle back, muttering, *"Ema Lelo, Eba Lelo."* Then he slowly entered into the river, looking down at his reflection, then up to the leafy canopy high overhead, all the time talking to himself. Or was that an ethnocentricism; was he not really talking to the river, whom he had addressed, as Mbuti do the Forest, as Mother and Father? There are lonely moments in a fieldworker's life, and that was one of them. To be that far away from something that is so close, and so rich and good, is for me the loneliest of moments. It is the lover separated from his beloved.

Kengé sensed that, and he came up to me, this time speaking in KiNgwana, and carefully constructed the following sentence: "This was where we are." He looked me in the eyes to see if I had understood, then gave the Mbuti equivalent of a shrug of the shoulders (a pout of the lips). He went back to where the youths were busy eating "war food" that I had never seen before, a reddish seed pod that Kengé said would give you enough strength for a whole day of hunting. He then talked at length about such foods, and as we set off for the nearest hunting camp, where we were to spend the night, he pointed some of them out, occasionally plucking a berry or nut for me to try. Most were not nearly as tasty, to me, as the nuts and berries I had known Mbuti use at other times. The three kinds of berries I tried were all rather bitter, but seemed to be slightly stimulating. Kengé avoided any reference to the Lelo until that evening.

As we were sitting around a fire, in a burst of KiMbuti that I could not follow well, having been away from the language for so long, he told the camp what had happened at the river. It was then that still more new information came to me, vital information I had never known before—amplification of half-thought-out ideas I once had, as well as new ideas. Again, it was all related to the context of the present, as though there had been no need for me to know it before. Once again I was unsure whether I was learning something that was old for the Mbuti but new to me, or something that was new, even to the Mbuti, relating only to the contemporary scene. Actually, much of it makes so much sense of all that I had learned before that I suspect it was always their way of looking at time and space. But before, when the situation was normal, one of general *ekimi*, there had never been any need to discuss it openly.

I had always been aware of the Mbuti focus on the present, in time and space, but it had never been expressed in my hearing other than in comments such as, "If it is not here and now what does it matter where (or when) it is?" Such a comment would have been made in dismissing some villager demand relayed to a forest camp, for as far as the Mbuti are concerned when in the forest, the villagers simply do not exist (until they want them to). Or such a comment could be used to excuse oneself for not having done something that needed to be done the day before (like repair a hole in a hunting net) or for having let an antelope escape during the hunt that very morning. The discussion would then get on to the more important topic of what to do about the hole in the net *now*, or how to deal with the *immediate* shortage of meat.

But now the concept was expressed more formally, more as a statement of a generally unspoken philosophy that I really should have known all the time. How wrong I had been, standing at the Lelo, to think of the past. Kengé knew that was what I was doing, and it was not what *he* was doing at all. That is why he said, "This was where we are," while I was saying, "This is where we were." Mine was a mistaken perception of the Mbuti reality: Things are never what they were, they are always whatever they are, and that is the only reality we can deal with, or should try to deal with, the "now." And when Kengé paddled around in the water, looking at his reflection and at the trees above, one after the other, he was considering the nature of the "here."

As we sat around the fire I was asked if I had ever talked to my reflection in the Lelo, or ever touched it. I confessed that this was not the kind of thing that Oxford graduates did, though Oxford does give you just that kind of opportunity, if you are awake enough to take it. I was told to try it sometime, and given instructions on how to do it. Stand at the edge of the water, I was told, and look at your reflection. Who is it? It looks like you, but its head is down there, looking up at the other you. Is it thinking the same thing, wondering who you are? Then put out your foot, over the water, and gently lower it. The other foot will come up to meet yours, and if you are very careful (not to break the surface of the water) you will feel that other foot touch yours. You are getting to know your other self. Then as you lower your foot further into the water the other foot comes up, passes through your foot, and disappears into your leg. The deeper you go into the water the more of your other self enters into you. Just before you go right down into that other world, look down, and see yourself down there, all but your head. Only your other self's head is there. And then look upward as you go right under the surface, and you see nothing. Your other self has passed into the world you left behind, taking your place. Now walk across the bottom of the river, and slowly come out on the far side. If you look up from under the water you will see nobody, just the forest. But as you emerge into that world something will leave you, passing through your body down into the water. Now who is the real self, and which is the real world?

I would have liked a moment of silence to think that one out, but all the Mbuti burst into shrieks of laughter, as though I had been the victim of some great hoax. Really they were just laughing at my own stupidity for never having realized such a simple truth before; none of us are quite sure of anything except who and where we are at that particular moment. This is what Kengé had meant when he had talked to me about the years of war, when he said that the forest was no longer the same, that it had changed. But he was not making a statement about the future, which was how I tended to take it; it was not a "directional" change he was referring to. In any case his only proper concern was with the world as it was at that moment, and in that place.

One of the hunters cupped his hands into the form of a sphere and another pointed to the vaulted arch above us. From what followed it seemed that the Mbuti live not in a world of linear time and space, nor cyclical, but rather spherical. Ideally we should always be in the middle of our sphere. That is when there is *ekimi. Akami* comes from moving away from the center of our sphere. This can be done by moving too fast, with violence, in body or mind. If we do that then we reach the edge of our sphere and it does not have time to catch up with us. Give it time, and it will, but meanwhile, in that world of time (and until time stops again?) we are *waziwazi*, a KiNgwana word that denotes complete disorientation and unpredictability. People who are *waziwazi* are best left well alone. Give them time, their spheres will catch up with them; they will be back in the center of the world and they will be all right.

But if you are too violent or hasty (both among the most negative of values for the Mbuti) you may pierce the wall of your sphere. And as you pass through, like walking right into a river, something will come in and take your place in this world, as you enter the "other" world. That person will look like you, but will not be you. So if someone is *waziwazi* for more than a few days, it is probably not that person at all, but his or her other self. Then it is best to move the camp and suggest that that person go off and join some other hunting band. Perhaps the real self will find a way back, for neither self likes to be in the wrong world.

That somewhat lengthy discourse on Mbuti philosophy, given here in abbreviated form, is what they found necessary to tell me in order to help me understand their world at that moment. I believe that it is the way they always think, for it makes sense of the way they have been recorded to behave under different conditions in the past, and the spherical perspective of time and space does not deny continuity through what we understand as time, in a lineal sense. I think that if we are to understand the Mbuti perspective on change, and if we are interested in making any kind of predictions of how they might react to changes yet to come, we need to keep this concept of time and space in mind. And of course that comforts me, since it provides me with a ready excuse for not having discovered any of this on any of my previous field trips among the Mbuti!

CHANGING AGE ROLES

In that hunting camp, and in the few others I visited at this time (for my research project really was to do with the village world, as much as I would have liked to stay on in the forest), I noticed some other changes. The hunting fires were invariably lit by children. Before they had been lit either by children or younger youths. This was immediately explained as being due to the relative amount of *akami* at any time. Now was a time of *akami*, even though the war was over, so the forest needed the fire to be lit by children who are the purest, the closest to *ekimi*, since they have not killed yet. When there is *ekimi*, then younger youths, those who also have not killed yet (as youths sometimes do, on the periphery of the hunt, when they are approaching adulthood) can light the hunting fire.

I thought I detected a slightly different usage of the same kinship terminology I had noted before. There was the same use of a very few imported terms, such as the KiNgwana *semeki*, for anyone related by marriage. But whereas this used to be used to indicate a slight distance between friends who would otherwise call each other *apua'i* (sibling), it now seemed to follow the actual marital relationships. I also heard one KiBira term, common among the Bira, but which I had never heard used by the Mbuti before except when in a Bira village. It was *noko*, which among the Bira refers to a mother's brother (or male cousin of the same lineage). Here it seemed to be used loosely to refer to any relative, male or female, of a mother and of the same age level, but like *semeki*, it was being used to make a genealogical distinction rather than serving merely to define a degree of affectivity. Small though these departures were, they seemed significant, since formerly the Mbuti had refrained from making such distinctions. They had alway applied their five kinship terms (grandparent, mother, father, sibling, child) equally to anyone living in that hunting camp at that time, consistently referring to all members of the camp as their "family": *"apa kadi, 'pa kadi"*—"one camp, one family."

Such observations are fragmentary and inconclusive, but they assume some significance when one compares them with the past custom, on the one hand, and with the more detailed observations made subsequently by Harako, Tanno, and Ichikawa. All of these researchers suggest an even more fine differentiation of kinship in Mbuti terminology, to the point that they seem to be describing the

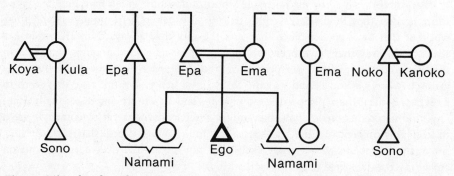

Fig. 8: This kinship diagram, drawn by M. Ichikawa (1978), suggests either a dramatic change in Mbuti kinship terminology (see Fig. 2) or else a marked regional difference. (Ichikawa obtained his information mostly from the region one hundred kilometers east of Epulu, where most of my information was gathered.) The difference could also be explained by different degrees of acculturation among relatively isolated hunting territories.

village system. Whether that is due to their observations being made in a village context or to a change in Mbuti perceptions of the form and function of family in the "new" forest context is difficult to determine. The Mbuti of course would say that a different "here and now" calls for a different kinship system, and with that most anthropologists would agree, though not many peoples we have studied are quite that flexible.

A NEW SURPLUS ECONOMY

In connection with the later studies of those same scholars, the almost casual observation that I made of an increased frequency of meat-drying racks also gains in significance. These were seldom seen during the colonial era, for the Mbuti were loath to hunt more than they could consume that day, such a surplus being considered as making for *akami*. But every camp I visited on this latest trip, without exception, had such a rack, and some had two or three. Clearly, I thought, they were trading more heavily than before with the villagers, something to be expected as the village population increased. But the Japanese ethnographers and John Hart, who is currently at Epulu, all indicate that the net hunt is much less efficient than it used to be. It is possible that even in 1970–71 the hunting was beginning to become less productive, due to the war, climatic change, expansion of the national park, or whatever. So it is possible that those drying racks were for the use of Mbuti as well as villagers, that they were beginning to have to save food for the next day, or against a time of hunger. If that was so, or is so now, then it would directly raise the question of *akami* as being related to overkill, and would demand a redefinition of that negative value. In this respect it is significant that not one of the above ethnographers make any mention of either *ekimi* or *akami*.

My visits to the forest, though necessarily few and brief, readily revealed such changes. This suggests that already Mbuti life, even in the deep forest, was being affected to the point that the process of adaptation was having a hard time keeping up with the pace and extent of contemporary change, and that something in the form of a social mutation was being called for. Events back down on the road directly related to the Mbuti and their forest world confirmed that suspicion.

The problem the Belgian colonials had faced when trying to induce the Mbuti to settle and farm along the roadside was largely one of incentive. It was easy enough to tempt them to make a show of trying out this new life-style, for the Mbuti are not unsusceptible to bribery. But to get them to stay for any length of time was another matter, for whatever the colonials had to offer, the Mbuti found that the forest had that much more to offer. The forest life-style was more to their taste: more comfortable, more healthy, more productive, more predictable, filled with more *ekimi* and less *akami*. The few luxuries the colonial or village worlds had to offer that the forest could not provide, as the Mbuti saw it, were easily had by barter or by "hunting," as the Mbuti called what the colonials called outright theft. And above all, there was no necessity for the Mbuti to change their life-style; the only pressure came from their own curiosity. The colonials, like the villagers, were unable to coerce the Mbuti, just as they were unable to persuade them. It simply was not worth the time or money of the administration to make any attempt to pursue the Mbuti into the forest and attempt physical coercion.

Following the years of war, however, this situation was subtly changed. The administrators appointed by the central government faced most of the same difficulties faced by the colonial government; the fact that they were African rather than European made as little difference to the Mbuti as it did to the villagers. But the villages had become more attractive to the Mbuti.

The years of war had spread *akami* throughout the forest. Even though the Mbuti did not suffer directly from the fighting, the forest offering them as much refuge as ever up to that moment, they did, for whatever reason, accept the villagers into the forest, and protect them just as the forest protected its Mbuti. They still kept the villagers at a distance, according to all the accounts I was given by both populations, but the distance was narrowed dramatically during those years. Further, while the villagers evidently stayed in hiding throughout the years of war, or at least during the worst of the fighting, the Mbuti seemed to have been able to visit the roadside with impunity even at the height of the war. This seems to have increased the Mbuti sense of security with respect to the village world, as well as in their relationship with the villagers themselves.

And as the village population increased, and the size of villages up and down the road was swelled by immigrant traders, roadworkers, shopkeepers, and government officials, the Mbuti found themselves more and more in a highly advantageous position. The traditional villagers, recently emerged from hiding in the forest, were almost as ignorant as ever about how to exploit that forest world for their own needs (the Mbuti had seen to that), and they were almost as reluctant as ever to even make the attempt. They thus depended on the Mbuti for forest products, as before, but no longer so much for labor, since cotton growing had been abandoned. The newcomers, though many of them did not share the traditional villagers' fears of the forest, nonetheless had not yet learned how to exploit it for their needs. So they too depended on the Mbuti for forest products.

The influx of traders and shopkeepers also meant that almost every village of any size at all, even some with as few as half a dozen families living there, soon had at least one store, and many had restaurants and bars. These amenities were primarily for the benefit of the road workers, administrative officials, and truck drivers carrying produce from one side of the forest to the other, for neither the Mbuti nor the villagers had ready access to cash. But whereas the villagers had little to trade, since the newcomers all cleared their own plantations, the Mbuti were able to sell their wares and purchase luxuries at will, without having to enter the labor market. All of a sudden, the road was a much more attractive place for the Mbuti, and their village camps began to take on a more permanent appearance.

The new government's attempt to settle the Mbuti had this working in its favor, and for a while it showed some signs of success. That was until the Mbuti found that living in the new style of roadside Mbuti villages affected their health seriously. It also caused increasing *akami* among themselves, as well as between them and their old village *kpara*, who resented the government's proclamation of the "*émancipation des pygmées*" as an accusation that they had enslaved the Mbuti. This situation was quickly to lead to a split among the Mbuti, some of whom saw in it a clear

The roadside is increasingly offering more incentives for the Mbuti to break with their past. Even the smallest village is likely to have a store stocked with attractive trade goods, offering to accept forest products (particularly meat and honey) in exchange or for cash. The poster on this store says Voter Vert, *or "Vote Green," the slogan of the ruling party. The picture is of the green manioc leaf, a favorite food throughout Zaïre, and thus a good incentive to vote. The symbolic color assigned to the opposition was red, "the color of blood."*

signal that they should all retreat back to the deep forest and cut themselves off completely from this new village world where there was now greater *akami* than ever before. Others, mostly the younger Mbuti, felt that they merely had to change their tactics and deal with this new situation by spending more time rather than less in the village world. An additional incentive for them was the establishment of government schools throughout the region. Until then the only education had been at the missions, none of which were anywhere near the central region. The Mbuti found these schools a great novelty, and with their usual insatiable curiosity the younger Mbuti were quick to respond to invitations to attend.

COMPETITION AND STRATIFICATION

Here another subtle development took place. The teachers at the schools I used to visit, on both sides of the Epulu river, without exception found the Mbuti children to be much quicker learners than the village children, particularly in language and elementary math. Within a matter of weeks it was not unusual to see an Mbuti child being used as a substitute teacher, readily and capably passing on whatever he had learned to village children. The new proximity that villagers had found with the Mbuti during the years of war did not make it easy for them to accept this demonstration of Mbuti superiority.

The Mbuti, on the other hand, were being introduced to a hierarchical world that was quite new to them, and were finding themselves in some ways in a superordinate position. The central government singled them out for special treatment, insisting that they were *citoyens* just as much as anyone else and must not be abused in any way. Teachers used them to teach village boys. They had more trading and buying power than villagers. And they were constantly being sought out and pampered by the immigrant villagers, who, unlike the old villagers, had so much to offer them in return for forest products. The Mbuti were entering a totally new (for them) competitive world, but without any experience of the radical change that competition would demand in almost every aspect of their traditional life as forest people, as hunters and gatherers. The Mbuti still thought that they had the forest as a refuge and could move between the two worlds at will. But hierarchy and competition were the antithesis of all their forest values, and their very will to move between the two worlds was, it seemed, affected.

The national park now established firmly at Epulu began to increase its activities, seeking to capture more and more game for export to foreign zoos. To this end they established headquarters in other villages and employed more and more Mbuti to act as guides and for other tasks in the forest that villagers were unable or unwilling to perform. At the same time they tried to ban all hunting, at least in the park area. There was considerable disagreement as to the extent of their authority, local officials claiming that it extended over the entire forest. The station at Epulu said that it would control the hunting and would also control all trading of meat, that the Mbuti were no longer to hunt except under the supervision of the station. This, of course, was quite unworkable, so the station merely set about reducing the amount of trading, allowing the Mbuti to hunt but forbidding them to trade. Even this was gradually relaxed, and the station contented itself with nominally banning the private trading of meat for about three months of the year.

This would have had little effect, perhaps, except that now a new kind of entrepreneur had come into this part of the forest, the Nande traders from the southeast. Some of these countered the attempts of the station to control hunting by acting as middlemen between the Mbuti and villagers. Some of them even established themselves with Mbuti hunting bands and began to move around with them, though this was exceptional to begin with. Unfortunately, from my position as a villager, that being the given factor required for the research at hand, I was unable to determine effectively just what this all meant in terms of the traditional values of the Mbuti, values that militated so strongly against overkill, against the acquisition of surplus, against the acquisition of individual power (in the form of either acquired skill or status), and against the pollution of the forest by the introduction of nonforest elements of any kind. Another vital question that needed to be asked was what was resulting from the introduction of a new sense of individual power and competition into a society that was essentially egalitarian in all respects?

The hunt seemed crucial to me in trying to estimate the extent and nature of the change that was taking place. How could the Mbuti, in light of their beliefs, rationalize the massive increase in killing of forest game for trade? They had always kept their supply of game to villagers to an absolute minimum, using it for the express purpose of keeping the villagers out of their forest, to protect its purity. But now they were blatantly killing for sale, and competing with each other as well as with the station.

The only clear and consistent story I got was that, in this southern stretch of the forest at least, where the national park was having its greatest impact, the hunting was not nearly as productive as it used to be. Mbuti hunters coming in from the forest to trade their catch told of much smaller numbers taking part in the hunt than used to be the case. Net-hunting bands, at their largest extension in the annual cycle of fission and fusion, could number as many as thirty house-holds (a high recorded in the Epulu territory); more frequently they were a little over twenty. They never fell below seven, except during the honey season, when net hunting was abandoned and each band split up into tiny segments of as few as two or three households. It was generally agreed that a net hunt simply could not be efficient with fewer than seven nets of approximately a hundred yards (maximum) in length each. Yet now that seemed to be a fairly average size for a net hunt, and I began getting reports of even smaller groups attempting to hunt with four or five nets.

In the colonial era, I had not once come across any band, among all those I visited, that even attempted to hunt with as few as five nets. But then there was no need, for there was not the same pressure to supply meat to an outside world, and the nutritional requirements of the Mbuti could be met perfectly well, at least for a month or two, without any hunting. There was no dependence on the villagers for vegetable products, as welcome as these were as luxuries; the forest gathering practices of the Mbuti were perfectly well able to supply the needs. I could not help but remember how I had noticed that now the hunting fire was lit by children rather than youths. The Mbuti had said this was because of increased *akami*.

Whether all this was due to destruction of game during the years of war, or to some dramatic change in game migration patterns that resulted from the apparent climatic changes, I could not tell. In the forest the Mbuti seemed to be eating as much meat as ever, and large quantities were certainly being brought down to the road for trade. Yet all indications were that the hunting technique was somehow changing.

My curiosity as to how the related values and religious beliefs were also changing was piqued by another change: a change in the nature of the excuses offered by Mbuti who failed to satisfy a *kpara* or trading partner. The usual complaint had been of "bad hunting," followed up with tales of evil *saitani* and animals from the "other" world interfering with the hunt or stealing their catch, excuses which to the villagers were absolutely plausible. The excuses were now essentially practical, such as the hunting nets being in poor condition, or the hunters careless, or the game simply not there. Whereas such excuses would have seemed implausible and would never have been accepted before, in this new post-independnce world they had a strange ring of truth about them. And the fact that I did not once hear an excuse of a *saitani* as having made off with the catch told me a great deal about the change in the relationship between Mbuti and villager.

RELIGIOUS RAPPROCHEMENT

The opposition that had always characterized the two populations, for as long as we have had record of the relationship, was still in effect, despite the forced flight of the villagers into the forest during the years of war. And it was still for the most part an opposition without hostility. But before the opposition had been complete, coloring all aspects of social organization. The years of war had reduced the opposition between the spiritual worlds of the two populations to the point where they saw them as at least complementary, if not united.

The villagers' fear of the forest, a fear rooted in the belief that the forest was filled with hostile spirits, if not a hostile entity in itself, had now been replaced by a recognition of the more tangible and material dangers of forest life. The dangers were equally real to both populations. But during the years of war it had become obvious that they were less menacing to the Mbuti because of their extensive knowledge of the forest rather than, as had been supposed formerly, because of their supernatural powers or their affiliation with the forest spirits. It even seemed that the villagers had come to accept something of the Mbuti belief in Spirit rather than spirits, reducing the opposition still further. This process, undermining the old opposition, was at work throughout the two years 1970–72, but only became truly evident in the latter half of that period.

In the same way, the Mbuti attitude toward the the village *nkumbi* seemed to change. They had always participated primarily for the political and economic advantages that it conveyed to them. They now joined also because of what seemed

In an Mbuti camp built near the edge of a village is a kumamolimo *marked by symbols from the three worlds: a flagpole with flag; village drums and an Mbuti-made bench for villagers to sit on; and the simple hearth that is the* kumamolimo *itself, with the traditional Mbuti stick seat beside it.*

a perceived need to come to terms with the villager supernatural and to acquire some measure of control in that sphere. Previously the Mbuti had dismissed the world of the village supernatural almost totally. They were able to do this because their forest retreat always enabled them to test and disprove the validity of village claims to supernatural power. If Mbuti got sick in a village, as they invariably did if they stayed too long, villagers used to claim that it was because the village supernatural was punishing them for defaulting in their obligations to the *kpara*, or that it was because they had been cursed by someone who had a grudge against them, or wished to compel them to their will. But the Mbuti knew from experience that all they had to do was to go back to the forest and the "curse" (or sickness) would vanish. During the *nkumbi* they had in the past often deliberately contravened the most sacred injunctions of the ritual doctors, thus consciously exposing themselves to the threat of death by supernatural sanction. But, they observed, they never died.

But now, after living together in the forest for some years, each population seemed to have acquired at least a limited respect for the supernatural of the other. The Mbuti had become a little less sceptical of the supernatural powers claimed by the villagers, the belief and practice of which was nowhere more clearly evidenced than in the *nkumbi* initiation. On both the Bira and Ndaka side of the Epulu River, and further afield, both Joseph Towles and I observed that the participation of Mbuti was now made an absolute imperative. This was voiced specifically in terms of a need, that I had never heard voiced before, for the supernatural of both worlds to combine in the work of protecting and purifying the boys. And this was the first time that adult Mbuti participated as teachers in the initiation camps, and certainly the first time that any first-generation offspring of an Mbuti mother and village father achieved such high-ranking office as did Katchelewa Bangama.

A neat opposition still persisted between the two populations in other spheres of social organization: The Mbuti were still essentially bilateral whereas the villagers were patrilineal. The Mbuti were still highly egalitarian and had no fixed rules of inheritance nor any clear definition of private property, while the villagers had both very clearly defined. The villagers were at a level of political organization that distributed authority according to lineage and clan, with the senior member of the senior clan as the "chief," however unclear the extent of his authority over the relatively independent and autonomous lineages might be. The Mbuti did not even have these pretensions to centralization. On the contrary, they still persisted in applying negative sanctions to any Mbuti who made any attempt to assert any kind of authority over others, even when this was done in the name of some village or administrative authority. It was enough, for instance, for the station to nominate Makubasi as *"Chef des Pygmées"* for him to become a virtual exile even from the Mbuti village camp, and most certainly from the forest hunting camps of the very Mbuti with whom he had hunted for all his life.

But the loss of what had been an equally clear opposition in the world of religious belief and practice threatened the entire structure, and by the end of two years of observation a certain direction toward a more parallel alignment of the two systems seemed evident. One of the prime forces at work was the presence

Ritual doctors from three worlds: Mandevu, from the old traditional world of the past; Dr. Joseph Towles, whose interest in symbolism quickly earned him the reputation (and role) of a ritual specialist from the world of the wazungu; *and Katchelewa Bangama, the first Mbuti to become a ritual specialist and hold office in a village* nkumbi.

of a common "enemy," the black *wazungu*, an enemy that seemed more threatening to both indigenous population than the colonials had ever been. Another force was the experience shared by both populations during the years of war, an experience of a common destiny, of mutual concern and mutual respect.

All of this should, we might think, have manifested itself in a most positive way, leading to cooperation and harmony, but that is not quite how it worked. Moving from a relationship of opposition the Mbuti bypassed cooperation, being first introduced to competition. If anything, the relationship between the two populations now became increasingly competitive, with a growing element of hostility. That hostility was tempered mainly by the much greater hostility both felt toward the outsiders who were flocking into the Ituri, but it was by no means eradicated. Even though the government failed to settle the Mbuti along the roadside and turn them to farming, like the villagers, the very attempt presented to the villagers the possibility that the Mbuti would be even more successful than they, for the

Mbuti would have both the forest *and* their plantations to exploit. Moreover, the government, in providing the newly settled Mbuti with houses, clothing, and all the tools needed for cultivation, as well as the seed to plant, was seen to be preferring the Mbuti over the villagers. And this even more than the fear of economic competition increased the hostility felt by the villagers.

ECONOMIC AND POLITICAL CONFLICT

Then the Mbuti began to suffer from the effects of this settlement program, mainly through lack of proper training in the special kinds of health practices required by sedentary living, but also because of work patterns that brought on heatstroke. The Mbuti at first blamed the villagers, whose hostility was in no way concealed, and there were even mutterings of certain villagers having cursed them. The extent to which the Mbuti believed they had been cursed was shown by the length of time it took them to decide to abandon the roadside villages and return to the forest. In some cases it was not long, but where village influence was the strongest it was sometimes a matter of weeks or even months, and during that time the Mbuti developed a wholly new hostility toward the villagers. This dissipated when they did eventually return to their old way of life. But even then complaints kept coming in that the bad hunting, which had never been known before the years of war, was due to the villagers, due to the fact they had been allowed to live in the forest with the Mbuti and had desecrated it by their presence, or had even cursed it. What had at first seemed like a rapprochement between the two populations was turning out to be rather different. The new rivalry and hostility was proving far more dysfunctional than the old opposition ever was or could have been.

It needs a much more intensive study of life in the deep forest, nothing less than at least one complete year in each of a number of hunting territories would suffice, before we can be sure just how far-reaching is the effect of all this change on the forest social organization of the Mbuti. Even then a number of bands would also have to be intensively studied in their relationship to the village world before anything approaching a generalization could be made. Piecemeal short-term observations of a few Mbuti here for a month or two, and a few there for another month or two, are not likely to reveal much of value, particularly given an evident increase in seasonal change.

Piecemeal though my own observations were, the *tendency* from all that I could observe was clear. The Mbuti still kept their worlds separate, living one kind of life in one context and another in another context, and to some extent had different rules of behavior in each. In a sense they extended this old technique of keeping others at a distance from them by cultivating a third mode of behavior when in the company of the black *wazungu*—administrators, traders, and store-keepers. But the world of the black *wazungu* was pervading all the Mbuti worlds equally, just as the black *wazungu* were physically infiltrating the forest more successfully than the villagers had ever done.

Both villagers and Mbuti were speaking KiNgwana among themselves in a way that had never happened before, and there was a definite loss of knowledge of indigenous languages among the youth of both populations. This is particularly significant since in the Ituri, as elsewhere, language was a major factor in perpetuating the perceived distance between the many tribal groups. Each language group saw in their language, even when it was related to neighboring languages, evidence of the separateness and uniqueness of their identity. In coming to share KiNgwana as a common (and mutually foreign) language, Mbuti and villagers were taking the first step in assuming a common identity.

Even the usually conservative Mbuti adults, now recognizing the complementary nature of the two belief systems, and to some extent recognizing the validity of the village supernatural, were ready to accept with little protest the changes of lifestyle and changes of values demanded by the youth. In the old days the *mangésé*, the elders, the "great ones," would have made a point of discussing such changes before accepting them, to be sure that the youths recognized the full consequences of what they were doing. But even the word *mangésé* was heard less often, just as the *mangésé* were less and less often consulted and sought out for advice.

Similarly, two terms of abuse that formerly were frequently applied by Mbuti to villagers were now seldom heard. These were (among the Bira-speaking Mbuti) *bambongu*, or elephant, and *bangwana* (the same term as that applied to the Muslim Ngwana people). Both of these were typical Mbuti references to "animals" that were destructive of the forest. Now the Mbuti, when referring to villagers, more often referred to them by the tribal name, or by the insulting term *basenji*, almost equivalent to our term "savages." While the *nkumbi* was working its genius in pulling all the populations of the Ituri together in common opposition to the new outsiders, it seemed like the years of war and the new context of independence had laid the grounds for the destruction of the functional opposition between Mbuti and villager, splitting them ever further apart rather than uniting them.

With contrary forces such as these at work it was impossible to get a clear picture of any direction in which the changes might be leading either the Mbuti or the villagers. If anything, it was more like being in the directionless space/time world of the Mbuti than the more truly directional world of the villagers. The most that anyone seemed to hope for was to be able to deal with whatever context they found themselves in at that particular moment and in that particular place. This would give the Mbuti an advantage, as did their continued mobility, increasingly limited though it was.

The Mbuti were also able much more easily than the villagers to avoid the influence of the missions, which by the end of 1972 were once again beginning to intrude aggressively into the village world. The Mbuti were in less need of such practical benefits as the missions had to offer, such as medical treatment and schools. (And even for the villagers this need was now being met more and more by the government.) Even where a mission had been established for a generation or more, as in several parts of the eastern forest, the Mbuti there did not show any sign of having been radically affected by their nominal conversion to Christianity, still reverting to their traditional way of life as strongly as ever once back in a forest hunting camp. Further, the old arrogance of some missions towards all things traditional and African did not sit well under independence, and under African rule it became less advantageous and politically expedient for anyone,

Mbuti or villager, to be allied too strongly with a mission. As an agent of social change the missions were, if anything, less effective than before, and in this region at least served more to reduce than augment the influence of the western world.

This left the Mbuti and their forest world more clearly than ever in conflict with the village world, for the only visible mission influence was to be found along the road and the Mbuti were not slow in pointing to this as evidence of the inferiority of the villagers, evidence of the same weakness that had made them such easy prey to the Arab slave traders, to Stanley, to the colonials, the Simba, the mercenaries, and the black *wazungu*. However much their own beliefs had been modified, and modification there certainly had been, the Mbuti could certainly claim to have shown no such weakness with respect to the *wazungu* world.

Unfortunately, this makes the possibility of their adaptation to the changing world even more problematic, and seems to point to the necessity for what ultimately may have to be a radical change in their entire life-style. It was not so much the seasonal change, the change in game migration or any increasing shortage of game, or indeed any other economic or political factors, that were driving the Mbuti to the brink of some form of cultural mutation. It was rather that they had critically weakened their defenses by merging their beliefs and practices to some extent, however small, with those of the villagers. In this way they undermined the very essence of the structural opposition that had enabled both populations to maintain their own ways of life and belief intact in the same environment. Yet even so, the Mbuti seemed to believe that they had proven the invincibility of their traditional forest way of life. This belief could only sustain them as long as there was enough forest left to provide them with a refuge when things went wrong, as things were already doing more and more frequently. The national need for political and economic development seemed destined to make sure that the forest would be less and less effective as a sacred refuge from the profane outside worlds of villager and *wazungu* in the very near future. The only option left the Mbuti then would be to stop being Mbuti and be something else, in another world and another time.

Conclusions

PROGNOSTICATION

It is nearly ten years since I last left the forest as I write this, and though we have excellent accounts of various groups of Mbuti from the team of Japanese ethnographers that worked there subsequently, it is still too early to predict the outcome of the process of change so recently set in motion. It is worth considering, nonetheless, just what the various possibilities are, and what factors are involved. If nothing else, such consideration is likely to inform us about the nature of the process of change in our own society, and some of its possible implications for us. The Mbuti are no different from the rest of us in that they have recently been caught up in a world in which the pace of change seems to increase almost daily. They differ in that for them the scope of change is much vaster than it is for us, and its nature totally different.

The seasonal climate described by Tanno and Harako for the mid-seventies, for instance, is quite at variance with that described for the colonial era, and experienced myself from 1951 to 1959. We need much more data before we can assess the full extent and distribution of this climatic change, however. Both Tanno and Harako attribute the annual process of fission and fusion to seasonal variation within the forest, but since there was no such variation in the past it is possible that even today other factors are at work in determining the various patterns of Mbuti nomadism. And it is important to remember that there is absolutely no valid reason why there should be one general pattern; there might well be as many patterns as there are hunting territories. Seasonal change may very likely be an important new factor affecting nomadic patterns, however, particularly insofar as it affects the movement of game and the availability of edible forest vegetable foods. Seasonal change will also affect the Mbuti indirectly, insofar as it affects the activities of major roadside communities such as administrative and trading posts, road work cantonments, lumber mills, commercial plantations, and missions. It will influence Mbuti movement by creating not only a seasonal demand for their labor, but also a seasonal incentive for them either to come to the road or avoid it. In both respects it will affect the Mbuti differentially according to age and gender, and this will in turn radically affect their heavily age-and-gender-structured pattern of social organization.

The change in size and character of the roadside settlements is much less questionable as a factor inducing change in the traditional Mbuti way of life. Prior to independence many villages kept goats as well as chickens, and thus had at least some source of meat other than from the forest. The years of war destroyed all livestock, and up to 1972 only a few villages were beginning once again to raise chickens, and that primarily for purposes of trade rather than consumption. This, together with the continuing increased in the number and size of roadside settlements, created a totally new demand for all kinds of forest produce, but particularly for meat. The new settlements also attracted the Mbuti's interest and had more to offer them than had the colonial settlements. In considering any change in Mbuti nomadic patterns we must take into account the nature of such roadside settlements—traditional villages, administrative posts, lumber mills, missions, or gold mines—as well as what they needed of the Mbuti, and what they had to offer by way of incentive or payment.

During the colonial era it was already evident that certain luxuries were on their way to becoming necessities. Among such luxuries, which the Mbuti could at that time still do without quite comfortably, were iron products (mainly paring knives, machetes, and spear tips) and certain plantation foods (stomach-fillers such as manioc, plantain, and, where available, dry rice). Other village products, such as arrow tips, cooking utensils, and clothing, were considered more as trade items than as luxuries. But recent reports indicate that for one reason or another a very real measure of Mbuti dependence upon the villagers has replaced the previously viable mutual interdependence. This is all the more startling when we remember that in the colonial era the villagers had *economic* need for forest products whereas the reciprocal need of the Mbuti was *political*, namely the exclusion of the villagers from the central forest.

One reason that the Mbuti are now becoming more economically dependent upon the villagers, if that is the case, may be that they are actually losing a previously self-sufficient technology. This is not necessarily to be "regretted," for the distinction between self-sufficiency and isolation is narrow, and the present trend may be an adaptive one. However, virtually all reports, published and personal, as well as my own observations in 1970–72, indicate that the hunt is a prime cause for this new dependence. The larger number of villagers and the increasing market for meat to be carried by the passing trucks to the towns of Kisangani, on one side of the forest, and Bunia, on the other, means that Mbuti have to spend more time hunting if they are to satisfy that demand. *If* there has been any decrease in game, or adverse change in the migration pattern, that would increase the time needed still further.

I do not quite follow the argument of Tanno and Harako that this reduces the amount of time available for gathering. Among the net hunters the women used to gather as the hunt moved from one site to another and while the men were setting up their nets, and among the archers the women were not needed on the hunt. Some other factor is at work, unless the same passion that Mbuti always had for village foods is being mistaken for need. It may also be that there is less vegetable produce available in the forest due to the major climatic change that seems to have taken place. The Harvard study will give us more detail specific to that area, at least.

Putting the rather fragmentary and isolated reports together makes a disturbing picture, one which seems to indicate that not only is there less gathering, or perhaps less to gather, but that the hunting technology (I can only speak for net hunting) itself is somehow being lost. Or perhaps it is deteriorating as it seeks to adapt, unsuccessfully, to a rapidly changing context. For instance, a zoologist recently reported that large animals break through the nets and smaller ones slip through. In my previous experience I seldom heard of large animals breaking through the nets, and was never with a band when this happened. Nets took far too much time to repair, and were hastily lowered if any large game was put up by the beaters. The most damage ever done was if a snared animal was not quickly removed, in which case it would try to chew its way through the net and might damage it with its horns. As for smaller animals slipping through, they would have to have been smaller than the smallest antelope, since the standard mesh in the same area was seldom more than two inches. Tanno (1976) gives the mesh as five to seven centimeters (two and a quarter to three inches). But then Tanno also describes a very different technique from that known to me earlier, asserting that the men stand *inside* the circle of nets (it always used to be outside), and that game is beheaded. (This would only have happened if it was a large antelope that could not be conveniently carried whole; killing was always by slitting the throat, even in areas where there was least Muslim influence).

He also refers to men lighting a hunting fire, *near the place of the first hunt*, and using the charcoal to smear on their faces and thus secure a good catch. This is very different from the hunting fires that I had seen lit by children or younger youths, not so much to secure a good catch as to lessen the act of desecration. The ritual described by Tanno is, however, very typical of village "medicine," something Mbuti used to ridicule.

Both Tanno and Harako make virtually no mention of women or men gathering on the hunt, yet that is when it always used to be done. Both indicate that the hunt lasts much longer than I had ever known it to last in colonial days. Tanno gives an average time of nearly eight hours. Harako cites nearly eight and a half hours, with an average of seven casts of the net, each day. This would have been unthinkable in the old days, when the hunt was away from camp no more than four or five hours, frequently less, and might have caught enough for its needs after the second, if not the first cast. And finally, whereas any net hunt that I ever saw took the form of a semicircle of men with their nets faced by a semicircle of women acting as beaters, with youths standing at either side where the two semicircles joined, sealing the most likely escape route, both Tanno and Harako indicate that the men outnumber the women, and with their nets form an almost closed circle, the women beating in through the bottleneck. To me this seems more like a variation of another technique used by the archers, who form a circle and send in a dog, or sometimes youths, to drive the game from the center outwards, where the archers kill it with bow and arrow.

These differences might be explained by the fact that both Tanno and Harako were working at the eastern extremity of the net-hunting area, where there would be greater likelihood of influence from the archers. And Tanno's description of the hunting fire certainly indicates village rather than Mbuti religious belief at work. This all raises the specter of there being so many variables at work (diffusion, acculturation, climatic and environmental change, territorial variation, as well as differences in field techniques and procedures, let alone objectives) that it becomes questionable whether there is any value in comparing these divers studies in an attempt to understand the process of social change. But if we are content, for the moment, with general tendencies rather than demonstrable "truths," then we can say that plainly by the mid-seventies the Mbuti, wherever they are observed, have for whatever reason departed from their traditional way of living.

They have also, it seems, departed from their traditional way of thinking, though here we can so far only go by what has *not* been said. The fact that men light the hunting fire, and at the site of the first hunt rather than near the camp where the hunt will first set out, is one indication of a significant change in values, as is the "medicinal" (village) nature of this fire. The absence of any reference to the values attached to the killing of game is equally significant, for it is most unlikely that competent researchers such as these would have missed such a connection unless it had diminished in importance or been totally abandoned.

And there is no doubt that village beliefs were infiltrating even the forest life of the Mbuti. It was not just in the village that the *nkumbi* became a part of the life of the Mbuti. Their increased participation in official, even senior roles in the initiation is significant enough, but before I left the Ituri I saw the *nkumbi* strongly influence several Mbuti *elima* festivals. The *elima* that I saw in the seventies were held in villages rather than in the forest, and I was told that this was from preference. It would have been out of the question, before, for an Mbuti *elima* to do more than perhaps make a sortie into a village and stay there a few days. But now they not only started and began in villages, but they built an *elima* camp at the outskirts of the village, in imitation of the *nkumbi* camp. The girls dressed in deliberate imitation of the *baganza*, the *nkumbi* initiates, and were referred to as such by the villagers. This happened not only at Epulu, where something of the sort might have been expected because of its medial nature, but even at highly traditional villages such as those of Kopu and Koki and Bandindikpe, on the Bira side, and two similarly traditional villages on the Ndaka side.

With this in mind, I cannot help but wonder if contemporary accounts of what verge on unilineal descent systems among the Mbuti are not further signs of recent acculturation, rather than, as they used to be, part of the pretense Mbuti always used to put up, when in a village, of adopting the village cultural patterns, thus effectively keeping the villagers ignorant of the forest pattern. While both Harako and Tanno insist on a much greater degree of lineal unity than I had ever found, that was never (for me) really the issue. Everyone belongs to two lineages and *can* trace descent through either, both, or neither. I had observed Mbuti to trace descent in the male line exclusively for the benefit of or in relation to the village world. Descent had no significant structural or functional significance in their forest world. The lineage never functioned as a corporate unit, except, perhaps, in the event of death, when those members of the dead person's lineage who were present in the territory at the time were permitted and expected to mourn for the first three days. This exception hardly defines the lineage as a corporate unit. And while both Tanno and Harako trace descent in various territories they studied, just as I did, they cite no evidence that the *Mbuti* traced their descent in the same way, nor that the kinship system or terminology was of any social significance in either the forest or village worlds of the Mbuti. This may well be because their objectives were quite other than the study of kinship. But since both researchers spent considerable time in the forest it seems clear from their reports that the Mbuti used the same terms of address and reference when in the forest as when in the village, and this alone would be evidence of change.

Another example of "negative" evidence of change that has taken place among the Mbuti in these past few years is that neither Tanno nor Harako mentions the role of song and dance as an integral part of Mbuti social structure. This is true, at least, in the publications available to me at the moment, though there may be mention in as yet untranslated Japanese publications. Nonetheless, it makes me wonder, for both the technique of singing and the structure of the music were directly, even obviously, related to the most vital elements of Mbuti social structure. Change in the one would surely necessitate change in the other—for as long as adaptation were possible, that is. Just as net hunting becomes unproductive when the number of hunters falls below a certain minimum, or in the absence of the necessary ratio of male and female, adults and youths, so does the net-hunting mode of song become impossible to sing under the same conditions.

It is plainly hazardous to make any "general" assessment of the scope of change from the reports available at the moment. Even with regard to the nature of change there is little that we can add to what has already been suggested. The most recent information certainly indicates that the process of adaptation has given way to the more drastic process of alteration, if not transformation. A centripetal series of adaptations, always related to a central focal point, has apparently given way to a centrifugal or helical movement outwards. And it looks as though the vital strand that anchored even the centrifugal process to that same core in the past has broken, that strand being the clearly structured opposition between the forest and village worlds, the sacred and the profane. If this has indeed happened then it is not only useless to bemoan the past, it is neither doing the Mbuti a service nor doing them justice. They themselves would be the first to describe such a romantic attachment to the past as being *waziwazi*, out of time and out of place, out of harmony with the real world all around us.

INTERVENTION: CONCERN AND RESPONSIBILITY

What then does all this mean to us, other than that in order to deal with the present we obviously have to have much better information than we have at the moment? That in itself is a starting place, for in almost any consideration of social change it is the very nature of our information to be fragmentary, gathered as it is at different times, in different places, by very different people with different objectives. A certain humility is required, with respect to our own discipline in particular. Any piece of anthropological research is out of date the moment it is done, and any attempt to generalize for major populations in the absence of a wider coverage than can ever be accomplished by a single field worker is bound to be unreliable.

That *caveat* by no means implies, however, that there are not things that we both can and should do. Just what those things are depends to a large extent on the interests and abilities of the individual, but I see in the above account a clear indication that there are both things that we can and should *do*, and things that we can and should *learn* from such studies, given their inherent limitations.

There is a lot of disagreement about "doing," particularly when it smacks of "social engineering." Ultimately, of course, the responsibility for "doing" lies with governments, but it seems clear that as scholars working in a foreign country we not only have an opportunity, but an obligation to contribute whatever we can to the work of minimizing the dangers of change, however induced. Whether we can or should attempt anything more positive is a matter of individual choice. Much less questionable, surely, is our responsibility to apply what we have learned in other cultures, from our experience of social change elsewhere, to the situation in our own societies.

And it may well be that abroad, as at home, the best way of becoming involved in the process of change, actively as well as theoretically, is through personal concern rather than academic interest. We may even set off for the field with a most excellently planned research project and find, upon arrival, that events conspire either to make that project impossible, or to suggest that there may be something even more important and worthwhile to be accomplished. It is at that point that our academic interest often becomes qualified (and, I believe, enriched) by personal, human concern. The balance between the two forces is not easy to maintain. Rather than argue the case it seems appropriate to give two examples that arose during the course of the 1970–73 field research undertaken in the Ituri by Dr. Joseph Towles and myself.

We were awarded a grant by the National Science Foundation for a study of the village population of the southern Ituri, designed to counterbalance the bulk of research that had previously been done on the Mbuti. My own research among the Mbuti had convinced me that to study the social organization of either population in isolation was only barely possible, but the only way to understand their dynamics was to consider both populations as comprising one total society. Even then I would have been sceptical about any boundaries defining that total society.

When we arrived in the Ituri, having made preliminary contact with the government of Zaïre in Kinshasa, where we discussed our project at length with the Minister of Culture, we found that there were virtually no villages to study. We informed the funding agency that this was the case, and that the best we could do was to observe the reformation of village society that seemed about to take place. The National Science Foundation could well have recalled us, but it was prompt in urging us to stay. Both the central and local governments also had to be alerted to our change in plans, and both agreed that this would be just as worthwhile, even more so from their point of view. They also requested that we keep them informed, since they had so few administrators in the field at that time. We both ranked that request far above any academic considerations that discountenance working as government "agents," even in an informal way. We made that decision in light of our impressions of the people we had met and who were directly concerned: the Minister of Culture and the Governor of the Eastern Province, as well as local administrators. The alternative would, for us, have been to abandon the project.

But our attitude toward cooperation was much more positive than negative. We were not being asked to help as "experts"; we were not being asked for any developmental plan ready to be implemented. We were merely being asked to help fill a temporary gap in the government's communication system at a highly critical time, when by any standards the area needed all the help it could get.

We also made the common courtesy call on the American consul in Kisangani, another formality deliberately avoided by some so as to avert any suspicion of being a government agent.

I mention these preliminaries because they are often treated as mere formalities, to be avoided or performed only perfunctorily, as though they were tantamount to signing some agreement to "collaborate." I have always found, even in colonial days, that such formalities often opened doors that could never have been opened otherwise, contributing to the scope and quality of the research. And just as often they made possible a cooperation that included participation of the society being studied in administrative discussions concerning their future. I have never once been placed in a position, as a result of making the closest contact possible with such authorities, where I could not readily refuse to divulge information if that seemed proper, and it has been seldom that I have had to refuse any request for information or action.

The two major considerations of the central government and of the local administration in the Ituri were economic and political. They were thinking at the wider, national and provincial levels, and had as yet had no time to grasp more of the local situation than was available to them through the old colonial records. Certainly they did not at that time have anything like enough trained personnel (or even untrained men and women who could at least have acted as observers) to study the economic and political repercussions of the years of war from the point of view of the Ituri population. (The Belgians had left their former colony with something like thirteen university graduates.) Their concern was more with the sensitive international borders with Sudan to the north, Uganda to the east, Rwanda and Burundi to the southeast, and Tanzania, just a hop across a lake.

They were also concerned that while this eastern province had never produced much revenue even for the colonial government, its productivity was now zero. The gold mines, coffee plantations, and lumber mills needed to be reactivated, the road repaired so that it was serviceable for both commercial and military transportation, a school system established (for the first time ever) that would reach into every part of the forest. And an administrative system had to be established that could effectively control such necessary preliminary development. This was at a time when the villagers had not yet emerged from hiding. There were still active rebels living like bandits in the forest; the road was all but impassable, and the administrative official nearest to Epulu had just established himself, under military protection, at Mambasa, fifty miles away (half a day's drive, if you were lucky).

From what I could see from the vantage point of living on the road, watching as villages slowly reformed, the political and economic considerations that seemed most urgent right there had nothing to do with international boundaries or the national economy. What seemed much more threatening and potentially disastrous was the mutual fear and suspicion that persisted while village society was slowly taking shape, and the severe food shortage and almost total lack of protein, vegetable or animal. The political situation gradually eased to some extent, particularly when talk began of a great *nkumbi* that would bind the forest together again. But mutual suspicion never died out entirely, and a big factor in this was the difficulty of communication. It was not just that the road was so bad that it was almost as quick to walk long distances as it was to wait for a truck to pass, which might not be for days. It was rather that there was little incentive for communication.

Ndaka and Bira villages had always tended to be somewhat isolated and autonomous, and the present conditions merely encouraged this tendency. In colonial days a market system had sprung up that helped solve both inherent problems—economic and political. Markets used to rotate from village to village, within clusters of four or five villages all within easy walking distance of each other. This provided an opportunity for socialization, for the resolution of disputes, for courtship, for entertainment, and for all the other needs that markets fulfill. It helped to link one end of each tribal territory with the other, and it forged links that bridged tribal territories. The unexpected failure or destruction of a certain crop in one place could at least be mitigated by market exchange. Specialists, though few, were able to offer their wares, and the products of blacksmiths, carpenters, potters, weavers and basketry makers, tanners, and others served as a kind of currency as well as supplying needs. The market also, incidentally, provided a vehicle for the movement of cash.

From the local point of view it seemed that markets were just what this part of the Ituri needed once again, and for the same economic and political reasons. Villagers themselves began recalling how well markets had served them, and Mbuti began to say how much *akami* would be avoided if they could bring their meat to markets rather than having to deal with individual villagers.

ECONOMIC INTERVENTION

Even when a request to intervene comes from the people you are working with, and where the need for some kind of intervention seems unquestionable, there can never be too much caution. In this case there were two anthropologists who could consult each other and cross-check each other's findings, and between us we could gather far more data than either could have done alone. We discussed the various possibilities with villagers from as far as the Ndaka *chefferie* to the west and the Bira *chefferie* to the east. We came up with a plan, the politics and economics of which appealed to everyone, even to the few Ngwana Muslims left in the area, which was surprising since the plan involved raising pigs. The project had to be inexpensive, easy to implement, and related in some way to the past. It had to demand participation and cooperation, provide economic reward, and directly affect each and every village along the roadside.

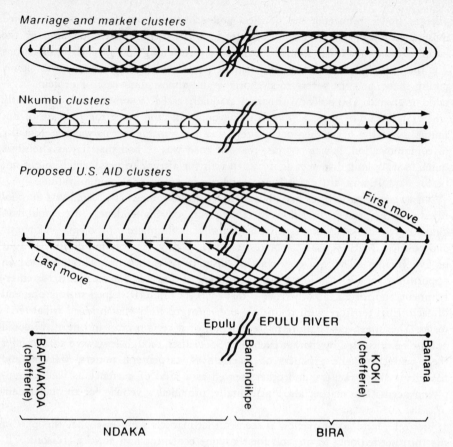

Fig. 9: Exchange patterns. This shows how the proposed plan for American aid would have corresponded to the traditional patterns of inter- and intratribal clustering and cooperation in markets, marriage, and nkumbi *initiation. See also Fig. 7.*

The authorities approved and offered to appoint local representatives to supervise the project until it stood on its own feet. The Mbuti, who might have been expected to oppose the plan since it offered the villagers an alternative source of meat, even offered to contribute some labor. (For them the connection with the past was that now, if the plan succeeded, the villages would once again have something worth exploiting.) (See Fig. 9.) And when the American consul heard of the plan he offered to ask AID (the Agency for International Development) for the necessary money, with no strings attached. It was only a small amount, but it would have serious affected our research budget.

The money was primarily for the purchase of hoes and axes for ground clearance, and for a small amount of breeding stock of a kind of hog well suited to raising in the forest. The plan was raise a number of hogs at Epulu, the labor being provided by the Ndaka villagers, with some help from the Mbuti. Epulu was chosen because it was the larger of the two medial villages on either side of the river,

Bandindikpe not having nearly enough people to initiate the project. Epulu was also favored because it easily fell under the supervision of the government agent at the park station. But the reason most often cited by the villagers for choosing Epulu was that it represented the best of the old days, since Putnam had always been a "chief" to both the Bira and Ndaka equally, and had always mediated on their behalf with the colonial government. The decision was acceptable to all.

Young hogs from the very first litters were to be set aside for presentation to the most distant village included in the project, across the river and on the far Bira side. That village in turn would present an equal number of piglets to the Ndaka village next up the road, westward from Epulu, and so on, until finally Bandindikpe would make the final presentation from its first litters to the distant *chefferie* of the Ndaka at the village of Bafwakoa. In this way the project would start at a village renowned for the Ndaka ritual specialists living there at the time, who would make the first presentation to a politically important Bira village (just beyond the Bira *chefferie* of Koki), and it would end with a presentation by the powerful Bira ritual village of Bandindikpe to the political center of the Ndaka. In this way the political extremes of the two tribal territories would be brought into an exchange relationship. And this was in an area where the social mechanism of reciprocity, with all its manifold implications, was well entrenched in tradition.

Meanwhile, the economic benefits, as well as the political benefits, would be felt locally as each village in turn became the nucleus of a small market cluster of villages. Epulu itself would be able to trade with Bandindikpe across the river, and the Ndaka villages to the immediate west.

All that the plan needed now to be put into effect was the land for the first hog farm, at Epulu. Sites had been chosen at all the villages, including Epulu, and there had been no problems, since with villages only recently established there was no shortage of suitable land where only secondary vegetation needed clearing.

The project collapsed before the first axes and hoes had even begun their work. The boundaries had been staked the day before, but in the morning, when clearing was to begin, the stakes had all been removed. A villager who sometimes called himself a Bira and sometimes an Ngwana (currently he claimed to be Bira), and who had recently established a small restaurant (which he claimed was Ngwana) on the roadside where the trail led down to the traditional village, appeared with an alleged kinsman who was a roving junior representative of the district administration. He said that the land chosen was his, that he was about to clear it to grow food for his roadside restaurant, which the government wanted to feed the government officials and *commercants* who passed by. And since it was an Ngwana (Muslim) restaurant he could not allow hogs to be raised *anywhere* in the village. Further, Mustafa claimed, his father had been Masoudi, the great Bira chief (actually a government-appointed agent, raised in a mission and then as a Belgian administrator's "house-boy"), and had acquired rights to this land in the days of "Putnam." He himself had been to a mission school, Mustafa said, and had powerful friends in government, like his "cousin" (the junior administrative assistant).

That was the end of the project. Something much more important than a viable market system had now come to the fore, and it was almost as though everyone had expected it. Mustafa's father had been a government-appointed *capita*, or headman, at a Bira village across the river, and had been heartily disliked by all. I had never thought of him as a "bad" man in any way; it was just that he had sold himself body and soul to the white *wazungu.* He always wore a white tunic with four pockets filled with pencils and other symbols of civilization. He had been one of the first that the villagers had pointed out as deserving of death at the hands of the Simba, and with him had died his wife and all his children, except for Mustafa. And now Mustafa wore what looked suspiciously like the same white tunic jacket and, just like his father, was behaving like an Ngwana while claiming to be a Christian Bira. And he was not even on his own side of the river.

For a moment there was an upsurge of hostility toward the Ngwana, still disliked for their association with slavery in the past and their subsequent association with the colonials, and, above all, feared for the supernatural powers they were believed to wield. Real Ngwana came to the fore and disowned Mustafa, and repeated that they had no objections to the villagers raising hogs. But the damage had been done. Even though when the administrator at Mambasa heard about it he recalled the junior who had sided with Mustafa and officially approved the usage of that land, nobody was prepared to risk being cursed by Mustafa. I was myself advised to stop eating at his restaurant, as I often did, in case I was poisoned. Word of this incident spread up and down the road, and with remarkable rapidity the entire project, which had been so enthusiastically supported, was obliterated by rumours of Ngwana treachery and threats of sorcery.

Blame was eventually diverted from the Ngwana, since there were not many left, to the black *wazungu,* and this, together with the *nkumbi,* was more effective in creating the political solidarity needed than the project could ever have done. The concept of reciprocity had at least been revived and remained alive; informal trading began along the lines suggested (mainly of plantains, sweet bananas, and manioc). Within a few months a regular market was being held at Epulu, though it tended to remain fixed there rather than shifting from village to village, as in the past. This was because of the growth of the station, and the trade goods which its members were able to contribute to the market. All that was lost, perhaps, was the advantage of shifting markets and a readily available supply of meat. Meat continued to be the major commodity in demand all along the road.

POLITICAL INTERVENTION

If "grass-roots" projects of this kind are subject to all manner of hazards, including inadequate planning, major projects imposed from outside are every bit as hazardous. Good intention has little to do with success or failure. President Mobutu's proclamation concerning the *"émancipation des pygmées"* did not fall on deaf ears in the eastern province. A well-meaning but uninformed entrepreneur, Lomata, took it upon himself to implement the proclamation by bringing the Mbuti out of the forest and settling them in roadside villages. There they would live by farming and, like other *"citoyens,"* make their contribution to the national economy and take an active part in the political process. His project somehow acquired official status and was given official blessing and financial support. At certain chosen sites he had clearings cut, and within a mere three months constructed "ideal" villages, much of the work being done by Mbuti under his supervision so that the clearing was efficient and the buildings, in the traditional rectangular plan of the local villagers, were sturdy and sound, fit for permanent habitation.

During this work the Mbuti were fed and clothed and supplied with all the necessary tools and materials. Sometimes cash incentives were offered to induce more and more Mbuti to come out from the forest and join these model "emancipated" villages. The actual numbers were small, but the effect was enormous, and far more disastrous than similar attempts I had seen made by the Belgian colonial administration. Then the Mbuti never had any real intention of staying; they had played along partly out of curiosity, partly for whatever they could get out of it in the way of food, tools, or other marketable commodities, and partly to please. As soon as these motives were satisfied they had simply abandoned the projects and gone back to their hunting.

But now there was more than curiosity. The material incentives were much more real and (now that Mbuti were also subject to taxation) tinged with necessity, and the desire to please others was replaced by a more materialistic self-interest. The project was, for the Mbuti, much more in the nature of a genuine experiment. It was clear to some of them, at least, that their world was already changed so dramatically that a correspondingly dramatic change in life-style was called for. Before independence there had been talk among the youths of spending more time down on the roadside, the better to know what was going on so that they could better adapt. Now the talk was of nothing less than abandoning the forest and becoming *citoyens*. Those that I spoke with refused to admit that this was the same thing as becoming villagers, for, they said, they would build better houses, have better plantations, make more money, be stronger and healthier and altogether "bigger" than mere villagers.

As I have said, the (for them) entirely new spirit of competition had already begun to infiltrate their forest world during the years of war. Now it began to emerge not only in assertions of difference, but in assertions of superiority. The villagers did not take well to this, since they had always tried so hard to assert their own superiority, though in a rather friendly, paternalistic way, and quite without giving offense. Lomata unconsciously fanned the flames, transforming the old traditional and highly functional opposition into a destructive hostility. He pointed to the new "pygmy" villages, which were indeed, while they were being built, neater and cleaner and better-built than any of the existing non-pygmy villages, and told the Mbuti that this proved that indeed they were citizens, and not just as good as anyone else but even better. The Mbuti, he said, were *real* citizens, because they were doing all this not for their own profit, like villagers, but to please President Mobutu and make their contribution to the new nation. The roadside Mbuti were quick to incorporate all this in their singing and dancing, which they were not loath to do whenever a single villager walked by to see what was going on, or whenever they visited a nearby village or market.

It was at this point that the villagers stopped calling themselves *citoyens*, a term that had assumed with great pride and satisfaction as the significance of independence began to come home to them. For the villagers the term, instead of being honorific, became a term of abuse and derision, an epithet far more filled with hostility, even violence, than the term "animal" had ever been before. "Citizens? Certainly not. *We* are *real* people. *Pygmies* are *citizens!*"

The villagers also saw what they took to be the government pouring money, not only into the construction of villages, but into the preparation of plantations for the Mbuti, with a seemingly limitless and free supply of the best of tools, equipment, and seed. They perceived this as a direct attack on their own economy, which was never much above a subsistence level, and at this time, just after the years of war, was still precarious and fraught with danger. The Mbuti, ever quick to ridicule such attitudes, countered with ridiculous boasts, which the villagers took seriously: boasts of how the government was going to buy only from pygmy villages and pygmy farms, of how pygmies were going to grow fat and wealthy and the villagers were going to die of starvation in their puny, dirty villages. Of course the government had nothing to do with any of this, but each division of the local administration seemed to think that Lomata's program had been initiated by some higher level in the local government, and at the provincial level it was assumed that it had all originated in Kinshasa.

In this way the new nation, almost overnight, lost the enthusiastic loyalty and all the vitality and fervor that had marked the first experience the village population of the Ituri had of true independence, of being a part of a free nation and of being asked to contribute to the growth of that nation. And while the Mbuti at first held the new government in high favor for all that it was doing for them, they had much less of any kind of conception of what a government was than did the villagers. In any case, disillusionment was not to be long in coming.

Also, notice, both they and the villagers had slipped into talking of *"pygmées"* rather than *Mbuti* in this new context. Even some of those Mbuti who had refused to come out of the forest and be part of *"émancipation,"* referred to the "emancipated" Mbuti as *pygmées*, or, also derisively, as *citoyens*. It is a poor day for a new nation when the very concept of citizenship becomes tarnished with derision, ridicule, and hostility, and when it is used to emphasize rifts between major segments of the nation's population.

Throughout all of this, Dr. Towles and I watched with dismay, but without interfering with as much as an opinion. The model villages were much closer to where I was than to the far side of the Ituri, where he was working. But even there, far away from any road, the *"émancipation des pygmées"* was having its effect, and relations between villagers and Mbuti were deteriorating, just as was the reputation of the central government, which was held responsible. But then we began to get reports of sickness and death. Meanwhile I had visited Lomata in Kisangani, and during long discussions with him about the program had begun to suspect that however well-intentioned he was, he was very much an entrepreneur, unqualified, and not, as was supposed, a government official.

Dr. Towles and I then jointly and separately visited a number of the model villages and found a terrible deterioration from when we had seen them a couple of months earlier. The Mbuti had abandoned the rectangular houses, most of which were still unfinished, and were living in their own style of small, conical leaf houses, built behind the others or on the edges of the clearings. Accustomed to

The rectangular shapes and inflexible architecture of the conventional villages were so foreign to the Mbuti that even when they stayed on the roadside they lived in their traditional leaf huts behind the abandoned "model homes" only just begun. These new villages for "emancipated pygmies" quickly became death traps, breeding malaria, dysentery, yaws, and venereal disease spread by truckers up and down the road.

never staying in one place more than a month, the Mbuti had no idea of the sanitation required by sedentary residence. The model villages were filthy and reeked with the odor of decomposing garbage and human excreta, since nobody had thought to teach the Mbuti to build latrines, let alone how to use them, or to follow hygienic practices other than those appropriate for a nomadic life in the deep forest.

Disease was rampant, for not only were the villages filthy, but water supplies had become polluted. This was something else that was totally beyond the experience of the Mbuti, who can drink with absolute safety from any source of water in the forest. The change from a high-protein diet was taking its toll. And on top of all this the Mbuti were suffering from the effects of heat prostration, due in part to prolonged living out of the cool shade of the forest, and in part to the nature of the work now required of them. This was work for which their musculature was simply not properly developed, and which necessitated far more exertion of energy than the same work did for villagers of normal stature. This resulted in a buildup of body heat, which was exaggerated when the work was out in the direct sunlight.

Health was further deteriorating because these model villages fell prey to truck drivers who found it possible to exploit the Mbuti girls as prostitutes much more cheaply than they could the more worldly-wise villagers. Not many Mbuti girls allowed themselves to be exploited this way, but even so, because of their own custom of premarital sex within the Mbuti world, the venereal disease brought by the truckers spread rapidly among the village Mbuti, and even from them back into the forest. It was impossible to pinpoint any one of these factors as the cause, but the mortality rate leapt upward, and Dr. Towles and I felt an unanthropological compulsion to intervene.

Through the Provincial Governor we notified the central government with a simple, factual report. Far from being ordered out of the country for "interfering," as might have been expected from newspaper accounts of the sensitivity of the government to foreign opinion, we were thanked for our concern, and within three weeks an investigating team was sent out. The program was halted to give us time, we were told, to come up with an alternative program for *émancipation*. This we were not prepared even to attempt on our own, but we contacted the Wenner-Gren Foundation for Anthropological Research in New York, and in view of the urgency of the situation they immediately agreed to finance a conference at their conference headquarters in Austria, setting us ahead of their regular conference schedule.

It is normal to plan such conferences at least a year in advance; Dr. Towles and I only had something like three months. But at the end of those few months we assembled at Burg Wartenstein an interdisciplinary group drawn from Africa, Europe, and the United States, and including Zaïroise scholars and representatives of the government of Zaïre. It had been planned to include two Mbuti, but at the last moment the government decided that the long air journey, and such a dramatic change of environment and climate, involving two weeks away from the forest, would involve too much risk to their health. So we had to make do with statements made by Mbuti concerning the issue of social change in the Ituri.

The extent of the interest of the government was evidenced by the fact that the Minister of Culture planned to come himself, for the entire two weeks. Just prior to the conference, however, he was appointed to take charge of another ministry, and the new Minister of Culture, feeling unprepared, appointed one of the principals of the National University to take his place. Right at the outset the government made its position clear, that its participation was conditional upon our agreeing to work entirely and exclusively within the framework of its official and published political and economic objectives.

The first two days were spent examining just what this meant, and some of the scholars present were at first reluctant to accept any such restriction on their freedom. But then the obvious necessity for such a position led us to accept it as a challenge rather than as a restriction. From that moment onward there was nothing but a lively cooperation in the endeavor to find a way by which the perfectly legitimate goals of the government of Zaïre for the economic and political development of the Ituri Forest could be achieved with a minimum of disruption and danger and remain as closely allied as possible to the felt and expressed wishes of the local populations.

That cooperation itself was perhaps more important than the plan for peripheral (rather than central) development that the conference eventually arrived at. In this case at least, the usual mutual suspicion and antipathy between scholars and government officials proved totally groundless. The fact that the scholars were drawn from different disciplines helped, for it made it easy for them to accept the government officials for what they truly were, representatives of yet another discipline. In studying President Mobutu's *Manifeste de la Nséle* none of us found anything that raised any ethical or moral problems. And rather than being a drawback, the two-week time limitation proved a positive asset. It was coupled with the government's frank statement that if we did not come up with an acceptable alternative within that time then that it would have to continue with its program for *émancipation* as best it could. Even to the government that was unacceptable.

The plan we arrived at was a compromise, but it is doubtful if we would have done much better if we had been given two months rather than two weeks to confer. The plan recognized and did its best to avoid the physical and social dangers that we had seen at work under the old program. It anticipated other dangers and difficulties that had not yet even appeared. And, above all, it made maximum use of all the positive potential we could discover: in the people, their culture, their aspirations, and in the situation itself and the will of the government to deal with it. Our greatest mistake was not to allow for continued academic cooperation with the government, so that ongoing field research would have been an integral part of the plan for social change.

DIVERSITY VERSUS CONFORMITY: PROBLEMS OF GENERALIZATION

The two situations described above (that of the plan for hog-raising and village markets, and that of the "model pygmy villages" and the subsequent Wenner-Gren conference) are not intended to show how to plan and implement social change, a specialized art in which neither Dr. Towles nor I had any training. Rather, they are intended to show how, in the field, circumstances may demand a choice between involvement and dissociation. Sometimes that is a choice between human concern and the lack of it, between responsibility and irresponsibility. Either of the two situations might have been dealt with better by others, but others were not available when and where needed. At least through the concerned effort and involvement of two individuals good will and hope were engendered. The anthropological perspective provided the basis for a deeper mutual understanding than had existed before, and a few practical gains were made. And our research, far from suffering, was considerably furthered by our being brought into an even closer, and somewhat different, relationship with individuals and with the society as a whole.

In addition, both the government and a number of academics from different disciplines and different countries were persuaded that it was possible and worthwhile to join forces in the face of social problems. The Wenner-Gren conference was for all of us an exciting demonstration of how well different disciplines and a national government *can* work together, given shared and genuine human concern. At the end of that conference we all realized how much more *could* have been done had such cooperation begun earlier, and had we planned for it to continue into the future. In itself, that was no small gain.

What can we and should we learn from such a field experience; what does it mean for us in our own changing social context? This of course brings us to a consideration of the comparative method, or perhaps better, of the potential of comparison. Such comparisons can probably only be made at a very general level, but that does not diminish their value. In making such comparisons we are concerned not so much with specifics, but rather with the general principles at work in two or more societies. (And as we look at the process of change and adaptation in the Ituri several such principles seem to suggest that a critical reevaluation of our own situation might be called for.) We are not, however, looking for a theoretical model, which, properly applied to another context, will provide specific answers to specific questions. Rather, we are looking for a sharpening of our awareness and sensitivity.

This is not to say that more precise, theoretically valid structural comparisons are impossible, or even unlikely; in a sense that is little more than a procedural and mechanical problem. I am suggesting that much less questionable and more certain to be profitable is the juxtaposition of the two cultures with the express intent of finding questions to ask, rather than answers to preformulated questions. This process is likely to be a creative one, the full pursuit of which might seem to fall more within the realm of philosophy than anthropology. It was this very pursuit, however, that gave birth to the concepts of both sociology and anthropology in the Enlightenment of the eighteenth century, and we would be little worse than presumptuous in attempting to return to it. That at least seems preferable to social irresponsibility. Moreover, it is a pursuit that can be followed by student and scholar, professional and layman alike.

Another factor must be taken into account when we confront the problem of generalization, particularly when dealing with an ongoing process. The problem lies in the question of where we can, with justification, draw acceptable boundaries within which such generalizations will be both valid *and* significant. That factor is related to the inescapable fact of diversity. So far the tendency of those who have worked in the Ituri has been to assume that not only is generalization about all Mbuti possible (I have fallen into this trap myself to some extent), but that there somehow *should* be a considerable degree of conformity, and this despite recorded differences in language, hunting technology, and environment! Scholars who find their theoretical deductions challenged, even by facts uncovered elsewhere *and* at another time by other scholars, not infrequently dispute the facts. This is a remarkable academic truth that is by no means confined to the Ituri.

Yet everything we know about the Ituri tells us of the reality of diversity, and suggests an almost conscious effort to maintain diversity and prevent conformity. If the various populations of the Ituri have anything in common it may well be their common dedication to the principle of opposition without hostility, a principle that has enabled them to come together as a powerful political confederation. Why should the same not be true among the Mbuti, given their highly nomadic life-style, their strong territorial affiliations with each other and with such a diversity of village populations?

All this makes me question what seems to be our own very different quest for conformity, our unwillingness to readily accept diversity, and our association of diversity and opposition with hostility. As economic and political forces demand a higher level of communication and cooperation among the various populations of the Ituri they seem to achieve this by increasing the complexity of structural interrelationships at every level: domestic, economic, political, and religious. Yet the thought of becoming "one people" has not yet begun to arise. Even the *nkumbi*, which could be said to be the foremost integrative institution, functions powerfully to reassert and maintain the opposition between all adjacent populations, at least at an ideological level, while integrating them at a political level.

Perhaps this is something we should look for in our own society, however we define that term (that is, hemisphere, nation, state, community, or whatever). This seems all the more necessary since we, under not dissimilar economic and political pressures, while clamoring for unity and conformity (as though they were synonymous), are also subject to many tendencies to fission and diversification in all areas of social life. The Ituri has much to suggest about such tendencies, including the possibility that diversity and nonconformity, even fission, *may* for us, as for the Ituri, be blessings in disguise rather than signals of disunity.

OUR OWN CHANGING WORLD

At a very general level, I find the very romantic appeal of the Mbuti provocative when turning from them to our own society. When *The Forest People* was published, although criticized by some as being romance rather than anthropology, it had enormous and immediate appeal. Even if the whole thing had been a fabrication, this would have been significant, for good novels often succeed by filling gaps in the lives of their readers. But *The Forest People* made its impact, I believe, because the near-Utopia described rang true, and showed that certain voids in the lives of many of us could indeed be filled.

The foregoing account indicates that throughout the long period of change affecting the Mbuti, the least of their concerns have been with material comfort, wealth, or security. Even at this moment, caught in the middle of an economic pincer movement, they seem more concerned with the quality of community life than with economic success. They are still largely preoccupied with values rather than goods, and still see security of the most social kind in a viable, however adaptive and changing, value system. Is it this focus on quality rather than quantity, on Spirit rather than Matter, that makes so many in our society envy something about the life-style of these remote, pre-stone-age, but contemporary African hunter-gatherers? If so, then what does the relative lack of focus on values in our society signify? What causes it? What does it portend?

Juxtaposition of two social contexts can provoke many such questions. It can also raise questions about more specific aspects of social organization. For instance, the Mbuti concept of family is quite at variance with ours. That in itself is neither surprising nor significant, but the question it provokes in me is whether or not this can be related to perhaps correspondingly different concepts of sociality in the two societies.

The familial image of "society" for the Mbuti is much more of a reality than it is with us, though we still occasionally talk of the nation as a family, or even of a family of nations. But with the Mbuti the family, certainly during the colonial era, clearly established a model for social behavior. It was a model based on the lesson of interdependence learned during infancy and childhood. It was an interdependence of all those within the "family," regardless of age, gender, consanguinity, or affinity. The process of socialization was built on the strong affective bonds existing within the nuclear family. They were quickly aligned with the effective bonds of mutual interdependence, transcending the narrow limits of the nuclear family. Clearly with our traditional concept of family a very different process is at work, tending to narrow rather than expand social horizons, with an emphasis on individuality rather than sociality, on independence rather than interdependence.

Unfortunately there are no recent reports on the situation in the central area best known to me, so I can only properly draw on changes that took place up to the early seventies, the first few years following the "years of war." But even at that point a change was taking place in the concept of family, perhaps corresponding to the increasing social cohesion coming about between Mbuti and villagers, among other factors. It seemed that the nuclear family was becoming a more enduring institution. That is, it was not just the *affective* basis of the wider territorial, cooperative, interdependent family, but in much larger measure an independently *effective* unit. The family, in assuming greater importance at the nuclear level, was becoming a divisive institution. A study of how this relates to the changing economic and political context in the Ituri might well throw light on the significance of current changes taking place in our own concept of family and sociality.

The apparent change in the Mbuti concept of "family" seems clearly reflected in the changes of economic values that were already manifesting themselves strongly by the end of 1972. In the past these values had been focused on cooperation, equality, and interdependence, with an equable division of labor between both genders and all age levels. These values were now being steadily replaced by competition rather than cooperation, independence rather than interdependence. Although economic equality still persisted and was maintained by extensive exchange and sharing, the way had been opened to inequality. For one thing, the Mbuti now had ready access to cash, their first experience of portable wealth, making inequality possible for the first time.

More significant still was the related shift of emphasis from their old economic norm of adequacy to one of surplus. The surplus was sought not for their own subsistence economy, but rather for the sake of maintaining effective relationships with the ever-increasing body of villagers dependent upon them for meat and other forest products. Before independence a surplus of meat arose accidentally, a cast of the nets snaring more game than the Mbuti could use that day, the surplus being sent to the village. Now the surplus was actively sought, and ideally every hunt was intended to produce a surplus that could be traded for both economic and political gain.

Thus the Mbuti seem to be moving inevitably to a more competitive economy, in which individual success is both possible and acceptable. With us the tendency seems to be different, despite the high value we still nominally place on private enterprise, competition, economic independence, and individual success. While we still nominally resist state control, in an emergency all that seems to be forgotten, and not only the community, but even the individual increasingly demands to be taken care of *by the state*, voluntarily opting for *dependence*. Even a minor disability is all too often made an excuse for early retirement on a comfortable pension, although some individuals suffering from major disabilities, whether entitled to compensation or not, insist on continuing to "earn" a living. And while there are areas where there simply is not enough employment to go around, the amount of initiative exerted towards the often stated value of "independence" through self-support is hardly remarkable. In plenty of areas where there is a job market it is easy to find those who prefer (or find it more profitable) to exist on unemployment benefits. In the rural county where I live, for instance, there are unemployed people who live in comfortable houses with plenty of land, yet who would not even consider hoeing that land in a serious attempt to grow their own food. Just as the Mbuti are finding (for better or worse) a measure of independence in their individual lives, we seem to be losing it. Whether that means that we are also losing our focus on self-sufficiency and individual self-interest or not is another matter.

Juxtapositions in the areas of political and religious life can also be usefully made. The clear allocation of political power to Mbuti youth in the past would surely have rung a familiar chord in the minds of the youth of this country, who protested so successfully what they took to be the cataclysmic political policies of a gerontocracy that would not live to suffer the consequences of their own actions. But in 1972 the Mbuti, who always felt that since the future belongs to the youth of today it is for them, not for the elders, to make policy, seemed to be giving away to the location of effective political control in the hands of the adults. This occurred as economic considerations became predominant, and for the Mbuti, as hunters and gatherers, the economy was necessarily in the hands of the adults. This contributed to the overall breakdown of the old system of interdependence, for now Mbuti youth had no area of social responsibility of their own, and together with children and elders were becoming increasingly parasitic, from the point of view of "productive" adults. This led non-adults to seek, wherever possible, their own independence, political as well as economic.

But this tendency was still, at that time, being held in check by the old concept of time and space. This, as with so many hunters, defined both economic and political needs in terms of that particular moment and that particular place. While there were all these tendencies toward fission, competition, inequality, individuality, and independence, however, there was still no room for the systematic planning for these values that is built into our system. The concept of "progress" itself remained a virtual impossibility, for the "here and now" still dominated. Political relationships, although from an outside point of view determined more and more by adults rather than youths, were still largely contextual, and constantly shifting.

To some extent that may be true of us. With the threat of a nuclear holocaust undeniably real, global destruction being alarmingly well within our potential, some find the incentive to plan far into the future somewhat diminished. Others find it negligible and, rather like the Mbuti of old, live from day to day. But that particular time perspective was for the Mbuti structured into a totally consistent social framework. For us it is, for the moment at least, still out of kilter with the rest of our social organization, geared as that is to the linear concept of time and the related value of "progress."

In the Ituri the impact of change is perhaps most clearly seen in recognizable shifts in religious belief and practice, and this makes me wonder if the same may not be true for us. In the relatively short space of time that I was away from the forest, a mere eleven years, the years of war seemed to have brought about major changes in both belief and practice. The remaining Muslim Ngwana were far less isolationist (as witnessed by their willingness to tolerate the raising of hogs and their almost inconspicuous participation in the *nkumbi*). The Mbuti were on their own initiative bringing their sacred *molimo* into the villages whenever they saw fit, exercising a measure of supernatural control in what had previously been an alien, profane world. And the villagers were incorporating the Mbuti more fully into the *nkumbi*, giving them increased responsibility as officiants.

But at the same time the Mbuti words denoting the values of *ekimi* and *akami* were seldom heard. This may, of course, have been partly because I spent most of the time in the village rather than in the forest, though I tried to allow for this. But all my cross-checking indicated the same lack of reference in the forest world to these two values. This change was the more significant because another term in the same language (a form of Bira) was being used much more widely. This was *bongaisa*, the causative form of the word *bonga* (also just *bo*), meaning good. In the causative form it meant to make good, or cure. Formerly this had both material and spiritual connotations. Medicine "cured" an infected wound, and the *molimo* "cured" death, making it good. But now the word was being used to imply that other supernatural curative powers were at work, spirits rather than Spirit, and this was strictly in line with village religious beliefs. The old opposition between the forest and the nonforest had apparently lost its sharpness; the Mbuti no longer seemed to regard the forest as their own private, exclusive and sacred world any more than they seemed still to regard the village as entirely profane.

This convergence of the religious worlds of the two major populations undoubtedly corresponded to and facilitated the greater economic and political contact that was now necessary. It in no way obliterated the opposition, though perhaps it had taken a step in that direction. Given the overall context, however, that is no justification for supposing that the next step will be in the same direction. Up to the end of 1972 at least, it was plain that differences in religious belief and practice continued to support a vigorous and vital diversity of self-perception, while at the same time providing a basis for effective interaction, even integration.

Changes in our own religious belief and practice are much more difficult to assess. For one thing, we start off with a much greater diversity than the Mbuti, and the tendency seems to be toward ever-increasing fission, division, subdivision, and reduplication, as well as multiplication by the introduction of previously exotic religious systems from beyond the Judeo-Christian tradition. The first question posed for me by the juxtaposition of the two situations is one of clarification. Whereas, despite shifts in both belief and practice among the various populations of the Ituri, there is absolutely no discernible diminution of the intensity of belief or frequency of practice, I do not get such a clear picture in our own society. The problem is compounded because of the loose way in which *we* habitually define "religion." But insofar as a belief in Spirit, or some supernatural power, is an essential component of religion (as it is in the Ituri), then perhaps the diversity of outer forms of religion in our own society indicates a reversal of the materialistic trend noted above, rather than a weakening of "religion." The very multiplication of "cults" may well indicate a recognition of the absence of Spirit in the more formal, established religions.

Whether we examine the problem at the national level or at the level of the smallest community, our understanding of the Ituri situation suggests that we inquire into the relationship, in our own society, of practice to belief and, where we find a discrepancy, to ask why there is such a discrepancy in our society and not in the Ituri. Does this suggest (as do other comparisons in other areas of social organization) that we are subject to change rather than adaptation at certain levels?

At the very least, any such juxtaposition is likely to make the most opinionated of us, provided we retain our rationality, question such generalizations as pose an "either/or" situation, as, for instance, in the two contrasting opinions that the proliferation of "cults" represents the failure of religion, on one hand, or an increasing concern with spirituality on the other. The Ituri situation tells us that both may well be true, that spirituality is sometimes most difficult to find in the body of a great formal religion, just as it is often difficult, in such religions, to find the intimate and omnipresent interconnections in daily life between religion and politics, economy, or family found so frequently in "primitive" religious systems.

If a consideration of social change and adaptation in the Ituri leads us to a more critical appraisal of the implications of change in our own society, such a study will have been more than justified. The extent to which we can make useful structural comparisons rather than content ourselves with juxtaposition will vary according to our divers purposes. The same is true of the extent to which we can or should apply the process in reverse, seeking to understand the process of change in the Ituri through such understanding as we have of the process at home. In the former case we should learn to be highly critical of generalizations as to the direction in which change is taking us and whether that is right or wrong, good or bad. So, in the latter, we should learn to avoid the mistake of those who bemoan the "passing of the primitive" instead of accepting the reality of change and learning what they can from simple cross-cultural studies.

Indeed, we might do well to start by learning from the Mbuti that there is as little sense in bemoaning the past as there is in anticipating the future. Perhaps such an attitude, such realistic contentment and occupation with the here and now, is only possible in their particular context. But we can still learn from it. Up to the present this way of looking at the world immediately around them has enabled them and their culture to persist through an incredible length of time.

The indications are that they will continue to adapt, back and forth, for as long as there is a forest in which they can perpetuate a forest way of life. For despite a certain religious rapprochement with their village neighbors, the Mbuti (in the Epulu region, at least) still seem to regard the forest as the major repository of all that is sacred, thus making something sacred of their total way of life, even in the context of contemporary change. So intense is their devotion to the forest, or rather to "forestness," that even if the forest is ultimately destroyed by conscious exploitation of its economic resources or by haphazard and uncontrolled over-development, it would not surprise me in the least if the Mbuti were to continue to adapt, finding a new source of sanctity in the new here and now. That indeed would be a lesson we could all learn from, and it need in no way lessen the importance of the measured concern for the future that is so necessary in our own social context.

Juxtapositions of the domestic, economic, political, and religious areas of social life among the Mbuti and ourselves seem to suggest that the Mbuti are cautiously advancing into the dangerous waters of modernization, with its increasing focus on independence, competition, inequality, and material wealth. At the same time, we may well be advancing by tentatively stepping backwards into the well-tried primitive values of family-writ-large: interdependence, cooperation, and reliance on community (or state) rather than on self, on Spirit rather than Matter. Perhaps then, as with our concept of time and space, we need to revise our concept of progress. We need to look beyond our own narrow horizons for a better understanding of what is "backward" and what is "advanced," and to search in other cultures for more wisdom as to where our ultimate security lies: with a conglomeration of individuals or with a society that is also, in every respect, a community.

Recommended Reading

The literature on the Mbuti is not extensive; the following suggestions provide a representative coverage of different points of view from different times and places. None tell the whole story; together they begin to approach it.

Harako, Reizo, 1976. *The Mbuti as Hunters: A Study of Ecological Anthropology of the Mbuti Pygmies.* Kyoto University African Studies, Vol. X, 37–99.
A meticulous study of Ituri ecology and its social significance.
Ichikawa, Mitsuo, 1978. *The Residential Groups of the Mbuti Pygmies.* Senri Ethnological Studies, 1, 131–188.
A constrasting study of the Mbuti band as a virilocal, patrilineal group.
Schebesta, Paul, 1933. *Among Congo Pygmies.* London: Hutchinson.
———, 1936. *My Pygmy and Negro Hosts.* London: Hutchinson.
———, 1937. *Revisiting My Pygmy Hosts.* London: Hutchinson.
These three popular accounts provide unusual insight into early techniques of anthropological research in the Ituri, as well as substantive data.
———, 1952. *Les Pygmées du Congo Belge.* Brussels: Mém. Inst. Royal Colonial Belge.
A good summary of the author's massive four-volume study in German, *Die Bambuti-Pygmäen Vom Ituri*, with important additional data.
Tanno, Tadasi, 1976. *The Mbuti Net-Hunters of the Ituri Forest, Eastern Zaïre—Their Hunting Activities and Band Composition.* Kyoto University African Studies, Vol. X, 101–135.
A clear, concise account of another ecologically oriented study.
Turnbull, Colin, 1961. *The Forest People.* New York: Simon and Schuster.
A descriptive account drawn from three separate field trips, largely from an Mbuti viewpoint.
———, 1962. *The Lonely African.* New York: Simon and Schuster.
A study of the interplay between the forces of tradition and modernization in Africa with six biographical case studies from the Ituri.
———, 1965. *Wayward Servants.* New York: Natural History Press.
A more formal account of Ituri society.
———, 1978a. The Politics of Non-Aggression. *In* Montagu, *Learning Non-Aggression.* New York: O.U.P.
A description of the major conflict-resolution techniques employed by the Mbuti.
———, 1978b. Society and Sociality: An Expanding Universe. *In* Du Toit, *Ethnicity in Modern Africa.* Boulder: Westview.
Intergroup relations in the Ituri.
———, 1981. Mbuti Womanhood. *In* Dahlberg, *Woman the Gatherer.* New Haven: Yale University Press.
The role of womanhood and family as providing a basis for Mbuti values and structure.

Glossary

akami: "noise," in the sense of conflict; the opposite of *ekimi*

apa: the Mbuti's forest hunting camp

anyota: sacred society of the Mbo, the "leopard man" society

apua'i: sibling of either gender (rarely, in imitation of Bira usage, *amua'i* may be used for "sister")

Bali: village farmers, those having the *anyota* society

baraza: covered sitting place found in all villages outside the houses of important people or lineage heads

Bira: village farmers

black *wazungu*:   term of scorn applied to many African government officials

bonga: good

bongaisa: to make good, to cure

bopi: the children's playground, a small clearing found near most Mbuti hunting camps

bulé: empty, worthless

eba: father (sometimes *epa*)

ekimi: "quiet," in the sense of peace; the opposite of *akami*

elima: the premarital festival celebrating puberty, focused on first menstruation

ema: mother

endu: the traditional hemispherical Mbuti dwelling; also "home," almost in the sense of "womb"

kadi: one

karé: "fellow initiate"; more specifically, "brother of the knife"; used by those who have gone through the *nkumbi* circumcision initiation together

kitawala: the name given to or taken by a number of societies, generally anti-colonial in sentiment, whether such societies actually existed or had any connection with each other or not

kpara: patron (rather than "master"); generally used to designate the villagers in relationship with the Mbuti

kumamolimo: literally, "the vagina of the *molimo*"; the central hearth around which the *molimo* takes place

Lesé: village farmers

mabondo: palm wine

makata: the portable xylophone (each "key" carried and played by a separate player) sacred to the *nkumbi* initiation

Mamvu: village farmers

mangésé: Mbuti elders; literally, "the great ones"

mavi: excrement; also used as an epithet

Mbo: village farmers

Mbuti: general term applied to all pygmy hunters of the Ituri forest

miki: child

160

moli: Mbuti term for the leopard

molimo: the central religious festival of the central Ituri net-hunters; also used to designate the trumpet used in the festival; also used to refer to the mythical "animal of the forest" represented by the trumpet, and to the leopard or elephant sounds it makes

molimo madé: the "lesser" *molimo*, in which the trumpet sounds like the elephant; a major force in conflict resolution

molimo mangbo: the "great" molimo, in which the trumpet sounds like the leopard; held in connection with death

Nandé: village farmers

Ndaka: village farmers

Ngbetu: village farmers

Ngwana: specifically, Muslim village farmers, associated with the former Arab slave traders

nkumbi: the circumcision initiation festival held throughout the Ituri every three years by all except a few of the Sudanic village farmers

noko: mother's brother, a Bira term formerly only rarely used by the Mbuti, and then only when in the presence of villagers

pa: family; perceived by the Mbuti as "any living in a hunting camp (*apa*) and hunting and gathering together at any moment"

saitani: a village term, of Arabic origin, designating an evil spirit

semeki: a village term for any affinal relative; most often used for brother-in-law

Simba: literally, "Lion" (of which there are none in the Ituri); the name taken by the supporters of Patrice Lumumba in their continuing fight for independence following Lumumba's assassination

tata: grandparent (of either gender)

waziwazi: unpredictable; any unreliable state of mind or behavior

wazungu: a general term for non-Africans, particularly caucasians, but not exclusively so

Zandé: village farmers

Note: In giving tribal names, I have omitted the Bantu plural prefix, as in the text. The correct usage of these prefixes would make for unnecessary difficulty; we would have to speak of "one MaMbuti talking KiMbuti to several other BaMbuti about U'Mbuti matters."

An initial *M* or *N* is pronounced with a very slight sound, such as is often represented by "mmmm."